DRIVING WITH DVOŘÁK

AMERICAN LIVES

SERIES EDITOR: TOBIAS WOLFF

DRIVING
WITH DVOŘÁK

ESSAYS ON MEMORY AND IDENTITY

FLEDA BROWN

UNIVERSITY OF NEBRASKA PRESS | LINCOLN AND LONDON

© 2010 by the Board of Regents
of the University of Nebraska

"All in Time," by Ruth Stone,
from *What Love Comes To*, is used
courtesy of Copper Canyon Press.

"Exultation," by Emily Dickinson,
from *The Poems of Emily Dickinson*,
ed. Ralph W. Franklin, is used
courtesy of the Belknap Press
of Harvard University Press,
Cambridge, Mass., © 1998, 1999
by the President and Fellows of
Harvard College, © 1951, 1955,
1979, 1983 by the President and
Fellows of Harvard College.

Library of Congress
Cataloging-in-Publication Data

Brown, Fleda, 1944–
Driving with Dvořák : essays on
memory and identity / Fleda Brown.
p. cm. — (American lives)
ISBN 978-0-8032-2476-6 (cloth :
alk. paper)
1. Jackson, Fleda Brown, 1944–
2. Poets, American—21st century
—Biography. I. Title.
PS3560.A21534Z47 2010
811'.6—dc22
[B]
2009031273

Set in Quadraat Sans
by Kim Essman.
Designed by R.W. Boeche.

In memory of my mother
Mabel Frances Simpich Brown
1922–1996

I will arise and go now, for always night and day
I hear lake water lapping with low sounds by the shore;
While I stand on the roadway, or on the pavements grey,
I hear it in the deep heart's core.
                    —W. B. Yeats, "The Lake Isle of Innisfree"

Out of this, we come in the endless sadness of children.
                    —Ruth Stone, "All in Time"

Contents

Acknowledgments

I am grateful to the following publications in which several of the essays included in this volume previously appeared: "Changing My Name," *Prairie Schooner*; "I Am Sick of School," *Iowa Review*; "Anatomy of a Seizure," *The Journal* (winner of the William Allen Creative Nonfiction Prize); "Walls Six Feet Thick," *Arts & Letters*; "Summer House," *Laurel Review*; "To Tell a Story," *Image*; "Hiking with Amy," *River Teeth*; "War of the Roses, *Terrain.org*; "Private Bath," *Brevity*; and "Soft Conversations," *Isotope*.

Changing My Name

The name that can be named is not the eternal name.
The nameless is the origin of Heaven and Earth.

—Lao-tzu (571?–? BCE)

Even while the Psalmist is uttering "His name shall endure
forever," look at his fellow Hebrews, stoning each other to
death for daring to utter it! Shrink the Eternal into syllables
and you have idolatry, or inaccuracy. Or both. Yet the next
lines from Lao-tzu are:

> The named is the mother of all things.
> Therefore let there always be non-being, so we may see
> their subtlety,
> And let there always be being, so we may see their
> outcome.
> The two are the same,
> But after they are produced, they have different names.

I swear, though, my name lies down over the naked being
that is not my name and gradually bleeds its color in. Pull

the two apart and each blushes with the hue of the other. My name itself, even, is colored with the past. I am a war baby and a first grandchild, named after my grandmothers—Fleda Brown and Sue Simpich—who lived next door to each other and needed to be equally appeased. They and my mother wove a tight nest while my father was overseas. The name Fleda may have come from Fleda Vetch in Henry James's *The Spoils of Poynton*—my great-grandmother supposedly liked James—or from a children's book, *Elfleda the Elf*, that was still in my grandparents' library when they died. There were three of us on Garth Avenue—Fleda Brown, Fleda Brown, and Fleeta Stevens, my grandmothers' age, next door on the opposite side from the Simpiches. We called ourselves the Fleets, and we all were: thin, alert like deer.

It is the beginning of the year at Leverett School. I know my name is next in the roll call because the teacher hesitates. I am tense, embarrassed, my name exactly matching my awkward self. I am not a Marianna or a Jane, no matter how hard I try. "Fled (as in 'escaped')-uh?" the teacher's voice rises to a question mark. She has assumed a vowel between two consonants is generally short. Or she says "Frieda," seeing not the actual letters but what she expects to see. In the sixth grade I decide to use Sue, my middle name. All of us are transmogrified that year, growing new bodies, trying the same thing with our names. When I am thirteen, I go by Sue all summer at the lake, the same summer I go without my glasses to win the love of a boy named Lee with large, soft lips, who spends the summer with his parents at Ken-Thelm, a resort down the lake. I feel my way through a fuzz of trees all through July and August. I paddle down the lake, trusting my instincts to get me around the point, past the shallows. The last day, before we leave, the reason for my deprivation tells me he is in love with Judy Carr, whose family owns the cottage next to ours, because she is such "a sharp dresser." Indeed, she is. I cannot argue.

Fleda and Sue represented a genteel tug-of-war between my grandmothers. My mother's mother, Susie Pauline Rawlins Simpich, a member of DAR, family historiographer, would take me aside when I was older and suggest that I fuse FledaSue, so her Sue would not be lost when I married. The Professor Browns next door were perhaps too much for her intellectually, but she had distant relatives who sailed over on the *Mayflower* to become part of the few indisputable American elite, and she had John Quincy Adams as her direct ancestor. She had *Nec vi standum nec metu*—Neither Hesitation nor Fear—on a coat of arms. And a brick with a label varnished across its surface that proclaimed, "Made by slaves on the old Rawlins homeplace."

At four or five, I am so intimidated by Fleda Phillips Brown that I will not call her by her name, Grandmother. The name is her choice. Susie Simpich is Nana, a name I am told I invented before I found out that half the grandmothers in the world are called Nana. But I duck my head in front of my regal Grandmother. I cannot say that I think she is wonderful: at

3

the age of four or five I have no such clearly formed thoughts, but her presence—maybe I pick this up from my mother, who is intimidated by her—often leaves me breathless. Who knows how energy begins to collect, to turn people into icons? She looks a little like Eleanor Roosevelt, only prettier, the same weak chin, the same slightly yellowed iron-gray hair wound on her head. The same strength in the wiry body, the same conviction in the voice. "Say Grandmother," my mother says, and I duck my head. "Oh, you can say Grandmother," she begs, as if it were her fault. I pull away. But I sit on Grandmother's bed and comb her long hair while she reads to me. I stroke and stroke with the ivory comb, lost in her voice, in the privilege of her long hair.

She died when I was nine. I don't remember any words we ever exchanged, but I remember other small scenes, walking to the outhouse with her before bedtime at the lake, for instance. We would hear the owl, the disembodied voice of the dark come to get me, to pull me into the black lake behind us. It felt as if I could not stop the downward slope of the path toward the lake. "Listen, Fleda, an owl": I imagine she said my name, and that was what kept me from the lake, the night of the owl. Fleda and little Fleda walking to the outhouse within the radiance of the lantern. I see her at home in Columbia, wearing her apron, washing dishes in a pan in the long porcelain sink. I have just brought in a bowl of crab apples from the tree in the back yard. She dries her hands and takes it from me and sets it on the table. How nice the crabby little things can grow, how heroic I am to have rescued them from the birds. Just that, two Fledas smiling.

🚗🚗

Brown, however, rested invisibly on me, an unflappable, probably German name, although it shows up in many languages. I imagine the prototype Brown—singled out, others pointing at her hair, or her skin, darker than theirs, mouthing the difference and freezing her into synecdoche forever. Hollow the *o* in upper palate, lower the bow of the tongue, and it comes out an elegant "ow," as in Eliza Doolittle's practiced "How now, brown cow." Or the name on the mailbox at Central Lake for almost ninety years. Or Great-Grandfather in a photo on the beach at Grand Traverse Bay, standing erect in his suit, vest, and tie, "properly representing the state of New York," as he supposedly insisted. Or Grandfather with a limp from TB, rubbing down his leg with grease that he claimed helped, swimming almost out of sight down the lake with his earplugs in, deaf to the world, or sitting in his lawn chair writing all morning, then at his typewriter all afternoon, writing books arguing for Land Value Taxation. Grandfather, stopping me between the two cedars in front of the cottage to correct me on the use of "whomever" instead of "whoever," teaching objective case while balancing on his one good leg.

When I say the name, the myth of the Browns is absorbed into me and speaks through me: Aunt Cleone, bringing her own organically fed chickens and sprouted beans with her to the lake, Uncle Richmond, building his own cottage down the lake, running triathlons at the age of seventy-five, and my father, taking long weekend trips with his bike club until he is almost eighty, and beating everybody, hands down, in the dictionary game. Point to the hardest word, ask him to define it. If he has never heard of it, he gets it right because of its roots. I invest them all with the brains and character I want for myself. I set their ideal selves in front of me to get me where I want to go.

The truth is, my original name is dead forever. No worker in the dusty back rooms of the Social Security Office, or the Bureau of Internal Revenue is at this minute pulling out an old manila file, exclaiming, "Oh yes, there she is!" At seventeen, I traded Brown with abandon for another color, Gray. At thirty-one, I exchanged that name for Jackson for the next twenty-three years, although the marriage lasted only twelve of those. I've worn Jackson longer than I ever wore Brown. It is another Brown I am taking up now, the other fourteen- or fifteen-year-old, the one who took a different path, who was not so desperate for love and attention that she needed to grab the first boy to come along and attach herself to his name.

For women of my generation, adolescence was particularly terrible. Our mothers were not who we wanted to be; we who wished to become powerful modeled ourselves after men. But the pulling away from our gender was accompanied by the dreaded breasts, the dreaded period, and our unconquerable, wild yearning for what they meant. We were torn from ourselves, we wrenched ourselves from ourselves with a vehemence, even while having kids, one eye on the kids, one on the open road, where our fathers were leading the way, whistling. I am perfectly aware that Brown is my father's name. Maybe in readopting it I am overthrowing my mother again. I prefer to think I'm reclaiming the joint project of their young lives, in its original, before it got distorted—like going back to original Christianity, or to Hinayana Buddhism, or Wicca. I know this is not the truth, either.

I have two grown children and five grandchildren at present, another one on the way. I have books and articles and poems published with the name Jackson on them. I have decided to quit worrying whether people will recognize me in print. "Fly down, Death: Call me: / I have become a lost name," says Muriel Rukeyser's Madboy. I could be a new poet, with a new name. Every poem is a new start. I suppose I might have changed Fleda, considering how many mutations naturally occur in my mail: Felda, Fleeta, Freda, Reba, Redda, Fleita, Lita, Leeda, Cleda, Cleter. But it is Jackson I have decided to abandon eleven years after my divorce, eight years into my present marriage. I have been wearing it, letting it flap at the end of my name to avoid confusion, and to avoid the dozens and dozens of agencies, bureaus, brokers, and banks I would have to contact. I can't say exactly why I've changed my mind now. I had a thought, though, of my tombstone, Fleda Brown Jackson chiseled on it for what passes for eternity to the human mind—that name no longer signifying the old, anguished relationship but standing at the point of death for expediency, officialdom, like a Social Security number. I want to die as fully myself as possible.

I imagine other people filling out the Change of Name Form— a Brad becoming a Rambo, a Jacamaya becoming a Mary, a Bernard becoming a Brad. I imagine them all with Hollywood motives, less serious than mine. But then I see that the form allows for change of minors' names—young children losing their ousted father's name, gaining their cruel stepfather's name, a furious mother changing all her kids' names to her own. I invent stories, all worse than mine.

It costs fifty-nine dollars in Delaware to change your name, thirty-four dollars for the newspaper notice, and twenty-five dollars for the filing fee. The form simply asks for your present name and your proposed "new" one. Then—and this is the sticky part—you have to advertise your intentions in a local newspaper for three consecutive weeks and include proof that you have done this with your application form. I choose a paper in Middletown, as far from Newark as allowed. I am embarrassed, as if I were a caterpillar with a Plexiglas window cut into the chrysalis so everyone can see the tender workings of its transformation. I wish I could let the change happen without having to say a word, just go out one day and be Brown instead of Jackson. Read my poems, don't read me. I am cringing a little, my nameless being shifting like a baby in the womb, readjusting in response to outer pressure. I am shifting inside.

This is no small change. The first person I told, besides my husband, was my son, Scott. "Well, as long as you don't change your name to something besides Mom, I'm okay with it," he said. So far, so good.

Standard Oil becomes Esso becomes Exxon. Bernie Schwartz becomes Tony Curtis. Norma Jean Baker becomes Marilyn Monroe. Prince becomes The Artist Formerly Known as Prince. St. Petersburg becomes Leningrad and then St. Petersburg again. The Belgian Congo becomes Zaire and then The Republic of the Congo. Rhodesia becomes Zimbabwe. And Czechoslovakia! Even our little Newark started out as New Ark. As thoughts roil and pitch inside our heads and interior images slide in front of our inner eye, the exterior frame is also shifting, collapsing, and being built again. Speed up time, and even the mountains undulate.

It is the day I am to go to civil court. Driving through the last of the golden trees, I remember that tomorrow is the third anniversary of my mother's death. I see her standing over my lawn chair at the lake, joking with me, calling me

Mrs. Beasley, my then and present husband's name. "No,"
I said, "That's not my name." "Well," she said indignantly,
"It should be." In her day, there were rules.

If a person can choose her own name . . . I feel the hairline
crack opening up in my public self. It's scary to think I could
become Rebecca Allworthy, for example, or Sonia Valentine. Who would I be, then? And what am I now, halfway
between one surname and the other, known to everyone
by one and carrying the secret of the other? I sign Jackson
on the credit slip at the restaurant because it's still on my
Visa card, even though I know that name is no longer all of
the truth. What does it mean to say you have changed your
name? You can just do it, without the legal work. You can go
by a public name but keep a secret one for Social Security
and on the other main documents of your life. You have that
power. Yet finally, there is some continuity of self beyond the
name, beyond the change of body cells every seven years,
the change of height and weight, of political party and hair-
style, of health or sickness. New cells keep appearing, repeating their mantra, "This, this, not that." New thoughts
keep appearing, already dressed and dancing to the old invisible rhythms below the surface of consciousness.

I'm surprised by the formality of the occasion. I pass though
the metal detector and into the courthouse, its rotunda
echoing. I am directed to the Court of Common Pleas office.

I am a commoner, my cause is common. It is required that I plead my cause. I try to see myself as assured in the marble face of The State. The clerk tells me I can go upstairs to the courtroom. I climb the spiral staircase instead of taking the elevator, enjoying the depth, the height, running my hand along the gold-topped banister, up to the broad window over the city of Wilmington toward the harbor and the bridge. I want to sit on the bench in the hall and look out the window, but the black-suited attendant tells me I can go on in, which makes me feel obligated to do so. Courtroom 303 is not large but contains the accoutrements— two lawyers' tables in front of a spectator's area, and the judge's "bench," as it is called, high above, with large books and a water jug. On the right is an American flag with an American eagle at the top of its pole; on the left a Delaware flag with, sure enough, a Blue Hen—the University of Delaware's mascot—at the top of its pole. I am beginning to feel a little giddy with tension. There is a witness podium with twin microphones in front of the judge. I sit in the spectator area and commiserate with the woman sitting next to me about how low the seats are, like car seats set on the ground. From here, the judge could be a Titan, Zeus himself. Exactly as intended, I am thinking.

The court clerk has slightly damp hair and a cold. The attendant tells her she should be at home. "I had chicken soup for lunch," she says. "I'll be better tomorrow. After all, I've been sick two days already." I am in a novel, allowed to peer through simultaneous layers, from intimate to official. The child behind me kicks his feet up and down and repeats "judge, wudge, dudge, pudge" to his father. "All rise," the attendant says. The judge comes in, perfectly in character—white hair, black robe—and there we are, a handful of us, feeling for a moment our illusion of autonomy crumble against the immutable script of the law. One by one we are sworn in and told to sit in the witness seat. There is a mother changing her eight-year-old daughter's surname to her own. Shelly, a pretty child with long blonde hair and a white ski jacket on, heads for the witness seat, but the judge asks her to sit below and interrogates only the mother. I am wondering why Shelly is never asked if she herself wants her last name changed, but I assume she does, since she obviously enjoys the occasion. She and her mother are a pair, I can tell by the way she swings back and forth in the lawyer's chair below, as if all the words have been rehearsed, and now all she has to do is watch. "Have you tried to contact the father?" the judge asks. "Yes sir, but I haven't seen him since she was born. He has had no contact with us and has not supported her." "Has he ever acknowledged his paternity?" the judge asks. "No," she answers more quietly. Petition granted. There is a young Black man, arriving late, dressed in new black jeans and a black Nautica jacket, changing his name from LeRoy to something that sounds like Jaméil—the judge clarifies the accent mark—"for business reasons." The judge doesn't ask what they are. Petition granted. There is a woman changing her young son's

name because she promised his dead father's mother she
would. I can't follow the whole story. They are there with a
man she obviously lives with, maybe a new husband. She
and the man are huge, very fat, and the little boy is tiny and
skinny, wearing a miniature old man's cotton fishing hat. He
looks like their toy, the "judge, wudge, pudge, dudge" kid,
grinning in the oversized chair. Petition granted. There is a
red-haired woman who gives her reason as "divorce" and will
say nothing more. Petition granted. I am last. I have been
planning what to say, how to make my two minutes perfectly
cogent, as if I need to capsulize my life accurately, provide
the nuances, make it clear who I am, before God.

I put my hand on the Bible, the relic of truth, the old threat
of damnation. Yes, I'll tell the truth, the truth of my whole
life, give me a chance—the slow pains of recognition, the
bursts of joy, the wrenching of love, of sorrow—but there
isn't time, so I distort it into what can be delivered in a flash.
Like a name. I state my name. I seem to be reading it off
my Change of Name Form, in my head. "Are you changing
your name in order to defraud any creditors?" the judge
asks. *Sure*, I think, my mind giggling to itself on a separate
track: *I am here to tell you, Mr. Judge, I'm changing my name to
defraud my creditors.* On the other track, I answer what he
wants to hear, unsmiling. "Were there any children by this
marriage?" "Yes, uh, oh, no, not by THAT marriage." Now
I've done it; I sound like a reckless woman, all those marriages. What kind of mother am I who can't remember which
one produced the children? How fit am I to be allowed to

shift my life again? I try a smile that projects warmth, sincerity, and stability. I draw myself up in the chair. "Why do you want to change your name?" he asks. I lean slightly toward him. "I should have done this eleven years ago," I say, "but I was too upset, you know, to take it on then, all the forms to change." He smiles slightly, nods toward me. I have him, I think. "And I am a writer; I was a little worried about name recognition. I've decided I can work with that after all." *Work with that*, stupid way to put it, but too late now. It's over. He mumbles "Petition granted," as if it were a sure thing all along, which we both knew it was, but give anyone a highly restricted forum, I'm thinking, and she'll knock herself out to be all she can be within it, creating herself every second.

Each of us is separately counseled to go back downstairs to the civil office to pick up our certificates. The others are waiting when I get there, the two kids watching the computer screen savers dance in multiflora patterns behind us, begging to play on the keys. I am surprised at how elated we all are. We smile and joke while the clerk triumphantly pounds a gold circle onto each certificate and squeezes the official imprint over it. He signs copies. He gives me the original and five copies in a manila folder. I ask him where the Social Security office is, and since it is on my way home, I take on the first of my tasks.

I do that, and I get a new driver's license, too. I am floating between names all afternoon, showing evidence of who I am. I am called Ms. Brown three times. At the DMV, I see the computer screen as the woman erases Fleda B. Jackson and types in Fleda Brown, and for a moment I am sad for Fleda Jackson, who has stuck it out for twenty-three years, for her own separate hard-won self. I see her brushing back her hair, gathering up her notes, cleaning out her files. She asks me what I will need and puts those folders aside for me. What will she do without writing? What have I done? I walk down the corridor to the photo room, dazed, but on my new driver's license, Fleda Brown is grinning. It looks as if she had just been crying, and someone had said something funny that made her grin in spite of herself.

Fleda Jackson keeps flashing at me from magazine labels and letters, from voice mail and e-mail. Last weekend I gave a poetry reading in Kansas and didn't bother to correct anyone when I was called Fleda Jackson, over and over. After all, there were my books, solid evidence. I allow her to go on, skating out like Roadrunner over thin air for a while. She'll fall soon enough. I have the rest of my life. Years ahead of me, Fleda Brown sits on her deck, a withered version of the driver's license picture. She wants to laugh and cry at the foolishness of names in the face of the nameless infinite. But still, it is good old foolish life itself, its pickiness, that she loves, has loved. The right word. Exactly the right word, if she can find it.

I Am Sick of School

I remember school as nothing but misery. Probably my memory isn't fair, but the way I generally operate is to keep myself moving by chasing the ideal, thus dooming myself to failure, loss, and suffering. And in the so-called tranquillized fifties, as the poet Robert Lowell dubbed them, there were plenty of ideals available. I started the first grade in 1950, so I am almost entirely a product of that decade. You might think it was easier then, before the world grew intricate as a computer chip. From where I sat, in my bolted-down, pen-scratched wooden desk with an honest-to-god in-service inkwell, all students were white, Protestant, and basically nice. This was the Midwest. By 1953, we had Eisenhower taking care of things in a mythical place called Washington. The big war was over, and the little one, too. The American ideal had triumphed. The planet would last forever.

It was a tough spot to be in. I would have to dredge up the means to suffer from within. There was no TV—not for me, anyway, until I was thirteen—so my education was mediated only through my own private drifting imagination, perhaps not as colorful or quick as the twenty-first-century imagination fed by SpongeBob SquarePants and the Simpsons. A dull kind of imagination I had, made up of rearrangements and distortions of what I already knew. But still adequate to scare me to death. When I was five, my father dropped me off for story hour at the local library five or six blocks from our house. He was planning to pick me up after, but story hour had been cancelled: when I climbed the dark stairs, no one was there. I walked home, crossing busy intersections, not sure which was the right way, my mind crowded with imageless horrors. If I had had TV, maybe fear would have looked like Maleficent from *Sleeping Beauty*, or Scar from *The Lion King*—a communal shape and color, recognizable by many. Whether this is good or bad isn't clear, but my internal demons have always outstripped the ones I see on the screen.

What begins as my own history, then, becomes my spiritual state, defined by absence. Whatever I can't have, can't reach, or can't touch accurately enough to explain—such as the details of my life, subject to decay or change—becomes for me an almost palpable absence. Like a blind woman, I keep trying to feel its walls, discern its shape. First grade, Grant School, Columbia, Missouri. Miss Jones. There I am, a skinny, earnest, silly little girl, alert every minute for trouble. It's not how many circles, how many curved tails I place exactly on the line, it's the ones I slant, wiggle, or make too small that are the problem. At the optometrist's, even though I guess as carefully as I know how, I am given tiny, gold-rimmed glasses to fit between me and the rest of the world.

Second grade. Huge, waddling German Miss Longenbach. We've been rehearsing a play for weeks. Our parents are invited. My mother and my grandmother arrive at the classroom door, all dressed up in scarves and furs, an hour late. I've told them the wrong time. My face burns with shame, with sorrow. Also in the second grade, the furnace goes out in the building. We are wearing our snowsuits in class. I am standing up front in a row with the rest of my reading group, reading to the class. I desperately have to go the bathroom, but I am too embarrassed to break the formation. I wet my pants, thinking maybe my snowsuit will hide it. "What's that?" the girl next to me says loudly as urine dribbles to the tops of my shoes. The teacher sends everyone else to recess and puts my pants on the radiator to dry. I am numb, watching abstractedly as my pants slowly stiffen like a large, white dried flower. *Everyone else gets things right. Try very, very hard to be everyone else.*

Third grade—who is my teacher? I remember nothing of that year except the funeral of my best friend—what was his name? Freckled, dark-haired, son of the people who rented my grandparents' farm, sent to town for a better education. Frank. Frank Corneilson. One day we were walking to my house for lunch, a week later he was dead from measles.

There he is, lying in his coffin, his mother kissing him, wet and crooning with sorrow. I'm next behind her. From far off, where I'm floating, I notice how dark each freckle has grown against his white face. I am not learning what death is: I am learning how to stay back, to let absence work for me. I develop a real skill for it. I learn how to bundle up some portion of the details, to save in case I want to sift through them later like cues. Meanwhile, I wander around like the Fisher King through my own fog, rich as myth.

Fourth grade, fiery-haired Miss Jenkins, also my father's fourth grade teacher. She takes us on a field trip to the cemetery next to the school and shows us her headstone under the trees, one date already filled in. I feel there's something I personally should do, that I should feel more than I do, that I should give her life more of my attention, before it's over. But I am standing in front of the immutable past, the terrible future, each headed in a different direction. I am in the middle, small and helpless. That is the feeling I remember.

Though I should pause to say that in grade after grade, the teacher held up my paper to the class as an example of how to do it right. I remember that, but barely the feeling of it. What I remember instead are the random panicky feelings, the feelings of isolation, of loneliness, of confusion, that pierced me, drove me, changed me.

Sometimes love is adequate to bring on misery. When we moved to Arkansas, I was going into the fifth grade. Oh, my fifth grade teacher Mrs. Bonner, beautiful, Presbyterian, artsy. She read us *The Secret Garden* every day after lunch. I was pale, thin, little Mary Lennox, unwanted, crouched under the garden's tangled vines, hoping to be singled out, to be noticed at last. I was utterly in love. My friend Donna and I visited our teacher's airy, art-filled home, right behind Donna's house. I giggled with nervousness in the temple of the goddess. I wanted to be adopted. My longing joined up with a more universal longing that year: we girls turned equine, galloping across the ruts of the playground whinnying and neighing in our sleek bodies that were filling with a new, animal energy we could only call *horse*. We read *Black Beauty*. We were stallions and mares, according to our talents. Then I moved to sixth grade, to stolid, elderly Mrs. Keesee, and to dreaded math story problems. Too late for horses. I longed for Mrs. Bonner like a rejected lover.

Is it the same now? Do girls fall in love with teachers and horses? In the sixth grade, we stepped out onto a precipice—an unsuspected edge, a new cruelty. I say "we," and this is part of my myth. It is the comfort of the myth, that we were together in this, that the wild horses turned out to be indeed ourselves. Georgena put angel hair down Jay McDonald's back, a flirtation, however awkward. The itching humiliated him for days. I mention Jay because I was in love with him, too—unrequited, I was sure. Imagination moved inward, downward, into our bodies. Someone's parents arranged a supervised "dance" where we were to learn steps, which I couldn't get right. Nothing quite right. On a snowy day, we girls brought our Ginny dolls to school in shoeboxes made up like beds, extra clothes tucked in the corners. We played dolls at recess, but joking and self-conscious, now, in our dialogues. What did we want? To be somebody's girlfriend? Or a mommy? Or the wild horse, still throwing its head back, whinnying for us across the vast ditches of the playground?

What did I want? Junior high terrified me. It left me without protectors—dolls or teacher-lovers or horses—alone with a body that, more and more, refused to be ignored. Sure, I had friends. But in those days one's body was basically a secret even from them, a secret relegated to the dark, not announced all over TV and in movies and magazines. I tell you, few of us understood sex. We didn't quite get how it worked. We girls had only the movie in gym class of our upside-down-vase-shaped interiors to go by. Who knows what the boys' movie looked like? I cannot possibly exaggerate the terrible, enticing, shimmering unknown that lay in wait for me, directly in my path. It took no form in my mind, exactly. It was as hollow as the movie diagram. It might save me. It might drown me. How did I ever learn anything, with this at me day and night?

By extra credit. By threats and misery. And by events too large to ignore, that bore me away from my narcissistic self for a while. In Fayetteville, Arkansas, in 1957, when I was in the seventh grade, federal troops were sent to Little Rock to allow a few Black students to enter Central High. My friends and I were humiliated for Arkansas, for ourselves. Faubus was an idiot. The U.S. government was too quick to step in. In civics class, we were learning the workings of the three branches of government. Ohmygod, here they were, converging on our state capital.

The advantage of each particular misery is that it brings its own struggle toward remedy. We had to wear skirts to school, not jeans. I had my one precious "tight skirt," hips clearly outlined, but the rest of the time I wore full skirts, sometimes "circle" skirts, a full 360 of starched and ironed cotton or bright felt, sometimes with designs—poodles, dancing teenagers, rickrack—sewn on. I would dip my net-like petticoats in liquid starch and hang them, spread out, on the line to dry. When I was fully assembled, my lower half resembled an open umbrella. My legs froze. My body, invasion-proof from the sides, remained utterly vulnerable from underneath. Protected by a rigid social code, I was still exposed where it counted most. No wonder the sixties came next. It made more sense to loosen the social code, put on a pair of jeans and protect what's most apt to need protection. Already, Tampax was beginning to be marketed big-time. Laboratories were perfecting the pill. Maybe it would yet be possible to invent a life free of the burden of the body.

Here is what we did to each other in junior high: we passed around "slam books," one person's name at the top of each page. You were to write a comment about that person in the blank space below the name. When it came to you, you could read what had been written: "Cute," "He's stuck-up," "I used to like her but now I think she's gotten too wild," "Pretty, but she needs to learn how to fix her hair." You turned first to your own page, skewered by each "slam." We were obsessed with everything "queer," although we didn't know what it meant. If you wore green and/or yellow on Thursdays, you were queer. You snickered your head off if a teacher said "This seems very queer." Personally, I had no idea what any of this meant, but, like most, I pretended. *Everyone else gets things right. Try very, very hard to be everyone else.*

I have not said much about actual classes, since learning was, of course, only a necessary backdrop. No matter that some of us loved it, no matter that I went around speaking French under my breath, no matter that I loved the first attempts at essays, at talking about books and poems. Still, the social structure loomed as large as the federal government; learning was only local politics. When I failed an algebra test, my humiliation wasn't about numbers and lines, it was about my unworthiness in the face of my friends' success. When it was easy to cheat on a French vocabulary test, I did. Someplace in my brain, I'm still sitting behind Karen, whose paper I copied from, dull with misery, with the worry that others will know, with the surety that as the teacher looks over the class and says, "Some of you cheated on this test," she is zeroing in on me. It is fierce, relentless, social pressure that both ruins us and makes us better.

The Test is both horrible and satisfying precisely because it attempts to neatly package life's problems. What else in the world carries the pressure of the ideal in its very bones? Yet in general science, each of the multiple choices sneakily contains a nugget of the truth. And how finely should I dissect the question without losing sight of possibly revealing grosser points? In algebra, how much credit for getting the right equation but not the answer? What if I remember the theorem but can't figure out how to fit it to the problem? What if, miraculously, I get the right answer, but use the wrong equation? How important is the answer? If I can write dazzlingly well yet say nothing much, do I get the same grade as the student whose essay plods along but makes a good point? Do the means win out, or the ends? Under the Bush administration, students are tested half to death in order that No Child Is Left Behind. Not that anyone would willingly leave any child behind, but it's damn near impossible to know: (1) Where the front is, that we want them all to get to; (2) How we would define arrival at the front, if we did find it; (3) What we'll do if they can't, or won't, get there; (4) None of the above; (5) All of the above.

High school seemed to me a big multiple choice test. The teeming generalities of junior high began to separate into more permanent choices. When I entered Fayetteville High School, my history of school pointedly began to diverge from the history of school. There were the rejections: I didn't get chosen for Sub Deb, the exclusive high school sorority.

I didn't get chosen for Hi Si, the second-best one, until the second time around. I tried out for cheerleader and didn't make it. Probably I was too quiet, too vague, no matter how enthusiastic I tried to sound. I was chosen at last for Peppers, the large group of pom-pom-waving back-ups for the cheerleaders. I couldn't keep first downs straight, but followed the lead of those who knew. I could've cared less about the games, but there was a certain, almost animal, satisfaction in marching onto the field in letter sweater and purple pleated skirt, sitting on the bleachers in a row with the others, waving my pompoms at the right time, yelling "Push 'em back, push 'em back, waaaaaay back!"

I met Harry when I was fifteen, and here is where my story could just as well begin or end—with my clear separation from the group activity we call school, to the beginning of my singular, anguished, self-tutorial. Harry and I had both been in Mrs. Andrews's homeroom, only he was there four years before me.

She was the Latin teacher; I liked Latin, a language with no practical use, all dreaming and invention. Harry didn't. He had been one of those who never joined anything, who sat in the parking lot at lunchtime, collar turned up, smoking. Now he was going to the university just down the hill, the first in his family, studying to be a civil engineer. My bleached-blonde next door neighbor, Gail, invited me to come along on a "date" with Harry and his friend Blake. Here came Blake in his souped-up, stripped-down Ford. I climbed in. Harry and I "made out" in the back seat most of the evening. I can offer many and convincing reasons why the absences in my own particular life compelled me to grab hold of a man, early, to be kissed, to be held, why I chose a man who was too old to date high school students, who was tense, migraine-prone, smoked two packs a day, and who gradually became an alcoholic. Many of those reasons would be personal, but some would be about school, and about the fifties.

Try to imagine not yet imagining the sixties. Try to imagine us, almost hating our mothers for submitting to their pots and pans when the war was over, for returning from the factories to be good wives and mothers again. Try to imagine us also wanting, partly, to be like them. If you could look down the locker-lined halls of Fayetteville High School about the time I started wearing Harry's ring on a chain around my neck, you would see me in my starched white blouse, tiny colored scarf at my neck, wide black belt and circle skirt, hair fluffy from huge brush rollers I had slept in all night, leaving red pock-marks in my scalp. I would be Loretta Young, or Doris Day. I would flirt and giggle. What you wouldn't see is the lone, dark stream of fear and resolve running through me, the one that tasted of iron, that knew not where it was going. The other self, that believed we should follow our mothers, sent me, like so many of my friends, into the arms of men—me earlier than most—and dammed up the dark stream, for a time. When our younger sisters were turning their backs on the old ways and lighting up a joint, we were already changing diapers, feeling cheated—yes we did, even while loving our kids, our families.

Finally, with the ring around my neck, I belonged to someone. The ring itself was my anchor in time and space, the ideal and the actual swirling around each other, closer than ever to merging. It's hard to translate this into now. There were roles then, and the roles were more important than the figures who filled them. We all knew that. What mattered first was that you were a wife, a husband, a mother, a father. Whether you did it well, or happily, was not so much the issue as that you did it. You *were* the role. Secondarily, you had a personality. By this means, the culture remained stable: children had parents, people knew who they were. Who's to say if this was good or bad? What it meant is that from the time I put Harry's high school ring on a chain around my neck, I did not have to be alone with my complicated self. I could talk about dating a college man. Then, we were "pinned"—I wore his Acacia pin, with its tiny diamonds and tiny chain, fastened to the front of every dress, every day, like a war medal. There were steps to adhere to, and I was adhering, albeit early. I sat in study hall and wrote Mrs. Harry G. Gray III, over and over.

I should back up, because there were junctures where things might have gone differently. I was in love with another boy, a good student, excellent in math, nice and good-looking, a quarterback on the football team. There was another, homely and quiet, unnervingly bright, who invited me as his date to the annual Latin club banquet. And briefly, I worked for the school counselor, who made me suspect I didn't need to glue myself to some boy to be okay. If I could have been aware of each turn, if I could back up and play them through in slow motion to see how my route gradually shifted until the energy ended up roaring down one lane instead of the other, I might be able to come up with barriers, blockers, filters, to change things. If I could get back there. If the "there" I imagine has any connection to the actual one. This is another loss that goes into the soup-pot of the ideal— what I imagine as lost chances.

It wasn't exactly as if I took a divergent track: I took both tracks at once. I split myself into That Girl (not Marlo Thomas) and This One. Let us take That One first, with her terrible acne, very good and athletic body, space-age winged glasses, and a longing for love nothing could fill up, every boy a potential remedy. When Harry started hanging around the halls during basketball games waiting for her, she went with him, a little ashamed, a lot excited. He was not a bad person, but it felt gritty and wrong. Most everything about him—she suspected in her soul—was wrong for her, except that he held her, he loved her, and there was little chance he would change his mind. What she learned: how to shoot BBs into beer cans, how to fill a Zippo lighter and change its wick without spilling lighter fluid, how to French kiss, how to teeter on the edge of sex-but-not-sex, building the tension to a religious fervor, how to raise her bowling average, how to keep her two lives utterly separate.

But That Girl could hardly get free of This One so easily. This One carried home huge, well-organized three-ring notebooks, elaborate assignment books. This One studied late into the night for an algebra test, and occasionally, by sheer determination, made an A. This one got all A's in English, greeted every essay assignment with breathless pleasure while groaning "Oh no!" to her friends. This One giggled. What she learned: that while many friends were smarter, she could succeed by dogged hard work, that her internal compass, deeper even than the urge for love, was ever swinging, swinging, looking for true North. Maybe she knew what agony it would take to get there, if there were such a place, but didn't mention it to herself so as not to scare herself off.

Senior year arrived for This Girl and That Girl, equally. My father had lost his teaching job at the University of Arkansas, mostly because he refused to finish his dissertation. At the end of my junior year, we moved to Cape Girardeau, Missouri. By then, I was "pinned" to Harry. I was leaving my school, my town, my friends, my only love. I tormented my parents with sobs all the way to Missouri. I started school. It was a good school, better than my old one. I made friends quickly. I made good grades. But suffering with loneliness,

I came down with such a bad case of flu—such high fever,
I became delirious. I cursed at my parents. It was all their
fault. I needed Harry. He came. We walked down Broadway
and picked out wedding rings. We got engaged. Here are
two interesting facts: next door was Eddy, a boy my age. In
the fall, I walked over to his house a few times to work on
a school project. Gradually, he came to populate my fan-
tasies—just a little—it would be unclear which boy was
which—but it didn't matter, since I would transform them
into my endless, passionate letters to Harry. The second
interesting fact is that at Thanksgiving, I rode the bus to
visit Harry. Next to me sat a young soldier on his way to Fort
Dix. We started talking. We had our cigarettes and coffee
together, stool by stool, at the rest stop. Back on the bus, I
pretended to fall asleep against his arm. I imagined going
on and on with him, wherever he was going. How can I explain what I felt? Excitement? Desire? Look at me! I was like
a kitten burrowing almost by instinct into any warm fold of
cloth. But there was Harry, waiting for me in his parents'
Buick station wagon, and we got married in January, and I
went back to Fayetteville to finish high school.

This, understand, is the same seventeen-year-old who was
initiated that fall into the high school sorority at Cape Girardeau by kneeling and being fed raw eggs and crack-
ers spread with Vick's VapoRub, and being pushed down
Broadway in a grocery cart at two in the morning. This is
the same seventeen-year-old who picked out a wheat-sheaf

dish pattern, who was taken to the doctor by her mother to be fitted for a diaphragm. Who walked down the aisle in her long white dress, pretty nearly still a virgin, a hopeless ideal of a bride. This was January, between semesters for Harry. This was 1962. When I returned to Fayetteville High School after the wedding, the principal, the father of one of my best friends, informed me that I was automatically suspended for two weeks, the penalty for marriage in high school. Two weeks later, I was still ahead in most classes, having already covered the material in Cape Girardeau. You can find me in my senior yearbook only at the end, a rag-tag group of us standing together under a caption that says "New Students."

We are out of the fifties in that photo, but you wouldn't know it. I took a home economics class and, with a lot of help from my new mother-in-law, made a pale green checkered Donna Reed dress with tiny pleats at the waist. We lived with Harry's parents until I graduated. My grades were the best ever. School continued to offer its steel framework to keep me from collapsing inward upon myself. It didn't save me, but it kept me on the assembly line of its vast fifties factory, ticking off grade after grade against chaos. If there was fear, there was also geometry, with its parallel lines that would never converge; if there was worthlessness, there was also English, with its glitter of words, its poems like cradles to rest in. If there was loss, there was also history, where nothing is ever lost, if you memorize the dates. If there was passion, there was also gym class, with its volleyball coming down hard in my court, demanding all my attention.

I've been a student, and now a teacher, almost all of my life. I'm sick of school. I have always been sick of school. It scares me. Yet, I get up every morning, turn on my computer, and submit to its discipline as if Miss Jones, Miss Longenbach, Miss Teacher Unknown, Miss Jenkins, Mrs. Bonner, Mrs. Keesee, and all the rest I can name are leaning over me to check. I bend over the screen and let myself be pulled into a completely unknown future. The work feels awful and humiliating, I have to say. It is as awful as it's ever been. But there is the happiness that almost doesn't want to be mentioned, so dependent is it on the misery. They are the two sides of the moon, absence and presence. Or, put it this way: I am twelve years old. I drag my sled to the top of Jackson Drive, huffing and puffing vapor. My hands ache, half frozen, my nose is numb. Then I climb on. Not once, all the way down, do I think about my nose or my hands. I am almost in heaven, flying. I don't know how it will end, exactly, but the short run down is so unspeakably wonderful that I am willing to drag my sled back up, even after dark, again and again. I begin to like the climb. Anticipation begins to feel as good as the trip down. Better, maybe. It gets hard to separate them.

Anatomy of a Seizure

Ontogeny

Probably when my mother carried the blue-knitted bundle of my brother through our door for the first time, he was already brain damaged. I don't know. It was like my parents not to have bothered to help my sister and me understand what little they did know. My father says now that he worried from the beginning. Even in the womb, he says, Mark seemed to hold very still, then jerk unnaturally, as if he were having seizures. But then my father has always lived within his own inexplicable womb of worry. It is possible my mother's bad case of German measles when she was three months pregnant caused Mark to be born retarded—no one knew back then what damage German measles could wreak. It's remotely possible, however, that he was bitten by a mosquito when he was about three months old and caught encephalitis, with its high fever, which damaged his brain. "Your mother naturally prefers to believe this," my father would say, with his frightening way of objectifying feelings. No matter. They did what had to be done, changed diapers, cleaned up spills.

Anxiety I

What I remember is as vague and fuzzed with anxiety as the rest of my childhood. I was nine when Mark was born; my sister Melinda was six. Already we had moved to Vermont, then back to Missouri, where my father reluctantly finished up course work toward a PhD in economics. We lived in his parents' house while his economist father was off lecturing around the country. My mother's parents lived next door: a study in contrarieties, the academic and the business-man. When my father proved to be difficult, childlike, and socially impossible, my mother's parents stiffened against him, but with as much Christian grace as they could mus-ter. All of this seeped under my skin, started a lifelong war inside me. Nana would invite my sister and me over in the afternoons and rub something called "Baby Touch" on our legs to get the first signs of dark hair off. "Sandpapering your legs," my father would say, furious. She wanted us to be ladies; my father wanted . . . well, I don't know that he wanted anything but to go hiking, sailing, and flying kites. And sex with my mother. My mother wanted . . . well, her wants were pretty simple: a hot fudge sundae, a new vac-uum cleaner, a little approval. All she got was a mother who frowned at the life her daughter had let herself in for and pursed her lips at her awkwardness, her inability to sew or cook creatively. And she got a husband who mostly reacted, who made as few decisions as possible. Let her ask him to change his shirt, and he flew into a childish rage. Rage was his middle name. But when he wanted sex, he was all over her, purring. She naturally pushed away. More fights.

Description

Into this edginess, Mark was born, the third child, the only boy. I only remember the questions, the budding of a new kind of tension, his diarrhea, the dirty diapers over and over, the beginning of a life of diapers. Mark started out a handsome child, blonde and blue-eyed, fine bone structure. His thin body seemed intended to be strong. Until he was two or three, it wasn't immediately obvious to look at him that he was retarded. At least not much. I can't remember. Until the last years, except when he was having seizures, his blue eyes sparked with what seemed like the possibility of intelligence. I think he would have been very smart. As he grew, the antiseizure drugs made his gums swollen and red. His lips got fat from the pummeling they took when he had seizures. His chin and forehead became as scarred as a prizefighter's, his teeth chipped. His head seemed gradually to grow too large, the way it leaned to one side, bobbling on his weakening, thin neck.

He scooted around in a walker until he was maybe three; then he walked like a toddler, on his toes, his feet unable to lie flat. Gradually, his wrists also drew up, his fingers didn't want to uncurl. He was able to walk until he was fourteen. He got a bad case of the flu, I think it was, and when he recovered, he'd lost so much strength in his legs that he couldn't walk any more. He spent the rest of his life propped up on the couch, or flat in bed.

Anxiety II

Mark was going to have a spell. No one knew when, but they were likely to come on two or three times a week. It could happen at breakfast when he was sitting in his high chair, his long legs dangling below the leg rest. It could happen on a long, hot car trip to Michigan. For the few years he was potty-trained, it could happen when he was sitting on the toilet, so he had to be held in case he slammed suddenly forward. His seizures stand for my own private anxieties, my family's anxieties. Something was always about to happen, and it wasn't good. Something was going to break down, money would be gone, someone was going to get strep throat, my parents were going to fight, my mother was going to lie on the bed and cry, my father was going to rant.

To Seize

To take possession of, to arrest, to confiscate, to grasp. Beginning with blankness in the eye, a stillness, a kind of aura you could sense, a slight whitening of the skin. This was all so quick, but still, my parents would say "Markie's having a spell," before it happened. Actually, it was already in process, inevitable, the electrical storm begun. All his muscles would suddenly be strung tight; he would lurch forward from the waist, throw his head down and arms out in front of him.

He would be rigid enough to break. He would barely seem to breathe, his eyes rolled up in his head, his mouth open and drooling. If there happened to be anything in front of him, he would slam down on it as hard as possible. He would bleed. We would hold his head, we would put a cold towel on his forehead. We would wipe the saliva from his mouth and chin. He would hold his position, quivering with rigidity for minute after minute. "My god, I don't see how he can keep that up," my father would say, chewing on his tongue. There would be a hopeless desperation, and a kind of ironic distance, a survival distance. My mother would sometimes be the one to stroke with the towel, speaking softly to him over and over. She would almost be crying, but not—the terrible not, the not that wanders in pain's wilderness and has no one to tell. Mark appeared to hear nothing. Where was I? Anywhere, nowhere, wetting the towel, holding his head, or in my room trying to get through my algebra with the leftover parts of my brain. Did the seizures hurt? Possibly. Sometimes he moaned as if in pain. Sometimes he whimpered. Gradually, he would begin to soften, gradually to collapse. Color would return to his lips. He would be exhausted but calm, his circuits blown, like a person after electroshock, I imagine. He would sit quietly for a while, and it would be an hour or so before he was himself again.

Voice

There's a quality of voice that carries the weight of awareness within it. It's rich, steady, resonant. Actors can mimic it, but it takes a full and conscious life to have it. There's the thin head voice of the afraid-and-afraid-to-reveal-it; there's the breathiness of the utterly held back; there's the loud frontal voice, skilled at argument, that uses the body like a weapon at the service of the mind. The most unnerving voice, though, shoots upward from the animal center, the body crying out in its own language while the mind remains asleep. Mark would cry out now and then, a sudden bleat—the tone of which was pain, delight, frustration, or simply assertion of being—but unalloyed, bypassing the cerebral cortex, as if it emanated from the ragged ingredients of the soul before they figured out how to merge. The precious few times we ate in restaurants, my father would carry him in, a gangly, half-grown boy. He would be fastened into a booster seat, his bib tied. Suddenly he would call out to the universe as if he and it alone understood each other, a raven's cry, a beacon. How easily I disappeared, then, moving through the vacuum that would have been shame, had I not sucked all the life out of it. At night, too: a wail, a screech, a reminder of how dearly silence is bought, how quickly it can be taken away. As his voice deepened, it came up from a cave I imagined as dark, dank, full of all his slow, sodden years.

Treatment

First there was only Phenobarbital, before it began to lose its effectiveness. Then Dilantin, which never worked as well for him. And Celontin, which made him seriously depressed, crying, tense, so that was stopped quickly. Others I can't remember, all ground up with mortar and pestle and mixed in his oatmeal, or mashed vegetables. Sometimes, when a medicine was working less well, or when doctors were experimenting with a new one, he would have grand mal seizure after seizure. He would fling himself over and over into his own abyss, gasping for breath. Now, there's surgery, a bisection of the brain that disconnects the cerebral hemispheres, that can be performed on people whose seizures can't be controlled by drugs. Exactly the right metaphor, it seems to me: sever connections; compartmentalize the suffering, break it down into its component parts; don't let the excitatory neurotransmitters broadcast all over the place and overpower the inhibitory ones; don't let the dendrites react to what the axons are shouting. This, then that—each aspect completed and coming to rest within itself, not whipping on the others to a frenzy. It's a kind of enlightenment.

Iron Curtain

The seizure trembled at the center of our existence. It was the meaning of family: our concerted alertness to the helplessness in our midst, the vulnerable core of each of us—the bedraggled unloveliness we suspected lay at the heart of each of us—exposed: our anger, our selfish desire for this all to go away. We lurched from day to day inside the borders of necessity. My parents never looked up long enough to see what help there might have been for his care, for his expenses, until several years after I left home. Probably it was when he turned twenty-one that a social worker came to the house and explained to them the possibilities. As a child, I hardly knew there was a world out there. When my brother Mark was born, it was 1953. Ike was president, the Beats were beginning their underground surge against the man in the gray flannel suit. Nuclear bombs were being tested. Guatemala was invaded, to "liberate" the people and to fend off communism. Communism loomed as the great world seizure, ready to make its move at any moment. America's tension may have infiltrated our own, but how could I know?

Priests

If the seizure was the center of our existence, doctors were its priests, Dr. Patrick in particular—young, handsome, and sympathetic. My mother needed someone to notice her, a surrogate parent, ten or fifteen minutes of undivided attention in a small room. My father needed science, a cool eye, a dispassionate physician's assessment, to distance himself. Dr. Patrick was not inclined, however, to offer his prediction of the worst, and perhaps we were all grateful. We needed and needed, but what we needed wasn't exactly clear. We needed—if I can see from this distance what it was—a few medical words embedded in ongoing Godlike concern. We didn't want him to forget about us, to let us slip from his everlasting presence. We were taken to see Dr. Patrick at the slightest provocation, and we were sick a lot: earaches, colds, flu, sinus infections. The delivery car from Collier's Drug Store pulled up in front of our house several times a week. When I wasn't sick, I invented an ailment, or exaggerated its severity. Oddly, perhaps, I wanted to stay home from school: the tightly self-absorbed system of our household was more familiar, more comfortable than the outside world. Dr. Patrick represented the blessing of that outside world on our complexities, an omniscient understanding.

Potty Training

For the infant-fold diaper, one doubles the entire length of cloth, ending up with a tight little triangle. Then, as the child grows, one begins the initial fold not at the half-way mark, but only one-third down the rectangle, and the corners are not brought so closely together, leaving more room for the legs. Soiled diapers are rinsed in the toilet, flushing and swishing. They're wrung out and stored in a plastic bucket. Each time the lid is opened, the ammonia smell jolts into the room, stronger as the child grows older. Just when the whole process begins to seem tedious and awful, there's potty training. Even for Mark, after a long while. For several years, before he became weaker and couldn't get out of bed, he wore training pants. But when he couldn't get up any longer, he wore several diapers at once, not folded at all, but flattened out and tucked down in the front. Safety pins would get rusty and dull from urine and would have to be stroked across a bar of soap to get them through the layers of diaper. He would need glycerin suppositories every day to have a bowel movement: the house would fill with the odor. By this time, he was fully developed and had to be washed carefully each time, his pubic hair kept clean and powdered.

Normal

I was beginning to understand something about normality. Normality wasn't normal. It couldn't be. If normality were normal, everybody would leave it alone. They could sit back and let normality manifest itself.

So says the main character, a hermaphrodite, in Jeffrey Eugenides' novel *Middlesex*. Ah, those of us who grow up in "abnormal" homes are the ones to consult when it comes to worrying normality to death! We know exactly what it is, where it is to be found—at Little League games, Dad grilling on the patio, Mom headed off to bridge club—images always receding on our horizon. We believe with our whole hearts in *Saturday Evening Post* covers, in Ozzie and Harriet, in the rest of the world—the not-us—living their lives within a halo of society's approval.

Michelle was born in 1958. I was fourteen, Melinda eleven, Mark five. Michelle never knew Mark as a smiling little blonde boy, babbling his words. She doesn't remember him walking. To her, he was a large, thin, almost-man lying in a hospital bed in her parents' room, emitting random, eerie cries, terrible smells. Our parents—isolated people, afraid of the outside world themselves—couldn't help her find ways to explain him to her friends. Her isolation fed the dream of normality, as it did for all of us, and the horror of being stranded outside that dream. She told no one about her brother. She avoided bringing friends home. On the rare occasion when she did, Mark would suddenly cry out from the bedroom, and all would be lost. Once, on a camping trip to Kentucky Lake long after Melinda and I had left home, Michelle was put in charge of watching Mark, who lay helplessly in the tent, while our parents went for a sail. Some of her new campground friends came by and asked her out on their boat. She went. She was only twelve—having to admit to the existence of her monstrous brother in the tent was more awful than the consequences of leaving him alone.

Baby Talk

While we were living in Arkansas and Mark was seven or eight, his teacher Mrs. Laverty reported that she'd catalogued three hundred words he could say. A vast number. He was potty-trained and could say that many words. He could run with the neighborhood children, his own head bobbling far above them, lurching and laughing. "Tee-dah," he called me. There was a kind of hope, a belief in progress in the face of certain collapse. The doctors knew what they knew—for the duration of each seizure, oxygen to the brain was cut off, gradually destroying more brain cells. What was our hope made of? Of one good day, of word after word, for the record. I am coming home from school. Mark is on the couch. He has had a seizure but is now calm and beginning to perk up. His face brightens when I walk in. "Tee-dah," he calls out, and lurches toward me. I love him with the same old miserable love that's followed me since. Things can't be fixed. Nothing can be nice, or clean. I don't know exactly who I am, yet I am asked to be this person, this "Tee-dah," and so I am, the roiling of my mind quieted for a moment as I hold him and kiss the top of his head.

I can see my mother in his latter years, before he went to the nursing home, sitting beside his hospital bed in their bedroom. She keeps a tall stool with a back on it next to the bed, to save her own back. She's talking baby talk to him. She's worn out with trying to shift his weight enough to change his diaper, to clean him up. She's using the voice, the baby talk he knows. She's stuck there; he's stuck there; we're all stuck, seized, gripped. Those of us who can, pull loose and get out. Those who can't, stay with the sweet language of the past, that once had meant beginnings.

Nourishment
It doesn't matter how old he is here. He's fastened in his scratched, wooden highchair, tied with a rag to hold him more securely. He is being watched carefully for signs of seizure. The highchair, actually, is a good place for it, if there's enough advance warning to get a pad on the tray, because he's protected against falling. My mother's on one side of him, my father's on the other, to quickly grab his head if he

jerks forward. On his highchair tray are bits of pork chop and green beans, cut small as beads to prevent choking. He picks up a handful and shoves them in. Some miss. He throws some of them. He's fed some of them. He likes it when we're all at the table. He babbles. We are not unhappy. Even my father, who has ducked his head and repeated the prayer my mother begs him to say before meals, even though he believes in science instead. "Bless this food to our use and us to thy love and service amen," he's intoned for her, with his flat, ironic edge. My mother asks for the applesauce, content enough. What is happiness but the nest we make for ourselves out of the tangle of troubles?

Thelma

Thelma Smith is hired to help my mother when Mark gets too heavy to handle. Thelma, barely literate, lives in a miserable hovel on Olive Street with her drunken, abusive husband and her children, including one retarded son who roams the streets, dirty, whooping, and mumbling. Sometimes, she reports, one of her children is bitten by a rat while sleeping. Thelma's husband won't let her take birth control pills, so she hides them at my parents' house and takes one there each day. She and my mother drink Pepsi and watch soap operas in the afternoons when Thelma is supposed to be folding diapers or washing clothes. "Why don't you make her do what you pay her for?" we ask over and over, but they just keep sitting, two women in silent rebellion.

Rescue

(1) Mark is on the sailboat, happily dangling his hand in the water. He falls overboard. My father dives in after him, grabs his leg. My father's leg catches on a rope. They dangle there for a moment, both of them underwater. My father makes a superhuman lunge upward. They're both saved. (2) Mark is lying in a tent at Kentucky Lake. He is overheated, burning up with fever. My father carries him to the water and swabs him over and over with a wet diaper. He is okay. (3) He is in the nursing home. They call to say he's very ill, that he may not live. My father suggests that they give him intravenous fluids, which revive him so that he lives a while longer. My father writes me, "It is unfortunate that we prolonged his misery as long as we did." He says, "I recall at the nursing home, there was one young boy who was almost totally a vegetable, and could do nothing but lie on the floor and salivate. Why we insist on keeping such people alive is more than I am able to understand. If 'God' intends them to die, how can we interfere with his divine plan? But if 'God' intends someone to live, and we help him to die, then we are guilty of the gravest sin and probably will have to spend an eternity in a lake of fire (according to some idiots like Saint John, the author of 'Revelation')."

Consolations

We're coming for Christmas. We've driven eight hours. We turn onto South Garth, three houses from Nana's, but Mark's about to have a seizure. My mother says we should drive around for a while so as not to upset her parents. And so we do, and finally he has the seizure, and my mother pats his face with a wet cloth until he eases. We drive up the driveway. My mother makes my father honk, as if we had just arrived, as if we're all excited.

"They have a poor afflicted boy," Granddaddy often says to their friends, borrowing that evangelist word, taking our lives out of our own hands, as if Mark is a visitation upon us.

Nana sits in her chair, watching the Lennon sisters on the *Lawrence Welk Show*. She says she would like my sister and me to be like them. They're singing about love, but their harmonies sound to me like humming about nothing, the kind you do when your mind's on something else, or if you were being forced to hum at gunpoint. My Uncle Bob's perfect family is here for Christmas, too, with their perfect, fiercely Christian children. They tell us secretly that our father is going to hell because he's not a Christian. Mark is sitting on the ottoman in front of Nana. She takes his head between her hands. She concentrates hard, closing her eyes. She squeezes and says "Be Healed," twice. We hear her say it. I want to kill the Lennon sisters, smash their TV faces with my foot. I want to raise the ugly, bitter, and dark world in front of her and make her eat it, bite by bite. I want her to get diarrhea smeared on her hands, to wipe up blood, to open her eyes, to know who we are, who I am, with my hard knot of love and rage. Anger forms a glorious seawall against my misery.

Indications

Mark is lying in his casket, in his pajamas, a full-grown man, still soft-skinned and no whiter now in death than in the last years of his life. He's more carefully shaved than usual. There is only a small crowd here, among them a former teacher, a nursing home staff person, a few friends of my parents, and my sisters and me. Mark's been completely lost so many years that the minister can muster no anecdotes for his sermon, no personal comments, only clichés. So I am left with my own feelings, whatever it is I feel, mine alone, and with Mark alone, inscrutable for all his twenty-four years, mirror of my best feelings and my worst, dear child I have held and comforted, needing comfort myself, dear child I have hated, hating myself, dear child I have cheered on with every new word, pushing myself to achieve, achieve, not to waste a minute of my life.

Now, almost thirty years later, my sorrow still feels private, my personal relationship with it as silent and respectful as that moment in which I sat in front of the plain coffin, closed at last. Sorrow remains within me like a closed box, the contents of which I know so well there's no need to keep checking. Still, sometimes one wants—one deliberately opens the past and lifts out, one by one, its small, radiant objects. One suddenly thinks of sorrow with fondness, the way it keeps on being itself, no matter how it's been anatomized, analyzed. Sorrow is easy to love, actually, the way it asserts its own clear presence that one can't dispute, can't wish away, for the way it insists on being included, along with everything else.

Driving with Dvořák

Adagio

I'm passing through a river of violins, clarinet-edged, rolling like these Amish fields. Through the plain annunciation of the oboe. Wait. Now there's a soft wind—the winds, dominated by flutes, tensing, tensing, against the full orchestra that comes crashing in. "Turn it down, turn it down"—That's me, in my head. I sound like my mother in there, my tense internal voice that tries above all else to maintain calm. But I fight it, the urge to tame Dvořák down to Muzak. "The New World Symphony" is one of my father's favorites, going on in me forever, whether I turn it down or not. At the moment, I'm listening to heaven-knows-how-old a tape made from a record, scratching and popping.

It's 1999. I'm on my way to Central Lake, my dear lake, one of a small chain that opens into Grand Traverse Bay and then into Lake Michigan. To the now-dilapidated cottage my grandparents bought the year my father was born. I'm in my nice clean Honda, inside a life that seems, in comparison to my past, like a great sigh outward, an expansiveness. I measure my life by its connection to the lake. In the bad middle years, I stayed away, unable to bear the contrast, I think. Now here I am. I've been coming back for ten years, a very good sign. This year's no different from the past nine, I guess, except for the Dvořák. I picked it deliberately, something I wanted to go all the way through, this time. I take this as a good sign, too.

I'm going to meet Millie, veteran with me of those days in the back seat of our crowded and messy DeSoto, and Michelle, fourteen years younger, who has dimmer versions of this trip. And my father, who rattles around in the empty spaces of his own childhood, terrified to paint the cottage for fear that if he spends any of his money, or if anything changes, the universe will collapse into dust.

I have never really understood this. By all reports and evidence, his parents were loving: progressive but strict. Still, something has always lurked in their tall, dark-haired, athletic oldest son—a hunger, a fear barely controlled by a triad of the major compulsions: money, sex, and religion. (He's for the first two, against the third.) And sailboats, which released him temporarily from them all.

True, his marriage to my mother was lonely and often combative. True, he found himself taking care of a retarded son a good part of his life. But nothing quite explains his fierce chewing on his tongue, his flaring with deep violence if any of us suggests getting an estimate for having the cottage painted.

The violence has often been directed toward me, the one who's most often defied him. Once, for example, he observed that I was using too much Dawn in the dishwater. "Who's doing the dishes, you or me?" I retorted. He raised his fist, veins standing out at the side of his head, jaw working, almost in my face in the close, dark kitchen. "By God, I'll hit you," he yelled. I admit, we'd been arguing earlier, in the sailboat. But the reaction was extreme—and I was forty-four. As the oldest daughter, I felt, always, the full blast of his rage, the complex, dangerous connection between us that required this anger—from both of us. When I was younger, he'd rap me on the top of my head with his knuckle, holding back, holding back from the blow he'd like to deliver, I could feel it, his blow, full-orchestra, aimed at the universe. I played only a small part—the one who, at the moment, was breaking open the scab a little over his terrible old wounds.

So this is the music made of accumulation—of a hundred trips, it seems like—of what we longed for at the end of them, of the first cool air after three days of driving in the heat, of the first glimmer of lakes, of firs and birches, of the signs for sour cherries. Of my mother's will to live, to be happy, to have cherries against my father's protest, against my father's panic over the drain of money—and now, these days, over the slow drain of his life and the increasing loss of control of old age. It is the music of the accumulations of my life. I learned to walk at the lake. When I stand on the dock and look either direction, the inside of my mind's reflected back at me, almost invisible as something other than myself.

The motif of Dvořák's first movement breaks my heart, so I have been whistling it as long as I can remember. You are dancing a Slavic dance. For a moment, you raise your head, and that quiet phrase of transience and pain reaches your nostrils almost like an odor. It has the sharpness of the clarinet, which is why I like to whistle it. It starts out in a major chord, key of D, the first couple of times. Connecting phrases take it to other parts of the orchestra. It changes to the key of F, diminished chord. A diminished chord has no tonal center; it leaves you tense, nothing to hold onto. It moves up the scale, leads you, keeps you anticipating changes—south wind: allergies, storms, gusts; north wind: sun and good swimming. Central Lake is narrow and gusty. I learned from my father that you have to sail with all senses alert, watch the roughening of the water for a shift, ride it, let it take you a little farther, before you tack again. Indirection finally gets you where you want to go.

I left home at seventeen to get married. Almost exactly a century before me, Anton Dvořák, son of an innkeeper who expected him to become a butcher, left home at the age of sixteen. My father has no interest in art or poetry unless it's utterly referential, and the poems have strong rhythm and rhyme. (Ironically, music alone, cut entirely loose from referentiality, seems to reach down into his inarticulate core.) I'm a poet who seldom rhymes. I've won prizes; Dvořák took up the violin and won the Austrian State Prize, again and again.

My father, no Dvořák, was twice fired from teaching jobs, the second time because he refused to finish his PhD. His MBA from Harvard wasn't enough for the University of Arkansas to keep him on. He retired still an associate professor at a minor Midwestern university. Although he calls himself a worthless worm, I know underneath he's always considered himself simultaneously superior and a failure. Where he failed professionally, I've succeeded. I suppose this may have been my plan all along. I live miles from Arkansas, where I grew up, and in multiple ways, miles from my father. What I do with my life, how I think, is utterly alien to him. But then, as he often admits, he's always lived on a continent of his own, one I can approach only as a tourist.

Dvořák lived in America for three years. "The New World Symphony" was his tourist's statement. His own title was "From the New World," a slightly different perspective: a traveler's letter home, a musical version of De la démocratie en Amérique, Alexis de Tocqueville's attempt to organize in his own mind the alien hodgepodge called America.

Now, in my mind, it's 1956. We're travelers ourselves in this America, my family on our way north. In the faint light, we pack everything in the DeSoto and pull out onto Maxwell Drive, out of the heat of Arkansas in June. Every inch of the back seat area is filled with boxes and suitcases, leaving no foot space for Millie and me, a blanket stretched over the whole thing like a train berth. It will be another hot day. My retarded brother Mark's in the front seat, doing okay for now. We are elegant with travel, subdued. This is the best time, when you beat the day, get out of there, smarter than what you've left behind. We have everything we need: fried chicken and pimento cheese sandwiches are wrapped in waxed paper inside the tin lunch box. My father's listing what we might have left behind. We've forgotten Mark's toothbrush, but finally, after a long debate, we decide not to go back. My mother wants Sinatra on the radio. In 1956, The Voice had just come out with "Young At Heart," motivated by the changes in taste that were beginning to be reflected also by Perry Como, Georgia Gibbs, and others. A lot of white singers were covering Black artists' songs. My mother mostly liked Nelson Eddy and Frank Sinatra, in a dreamy way, like an adolescent, not so much concerned with the music as with the feelings it called forth in her. My father liked mostly classical, so what I have of him is Dvořák. And Shostakovich, and Tchaikovsky and the slow pain of Prokofiev. "Turn that awful racket down," my mother would say, her face wrinkled up in disgust. "It makes me nervous." When she was out of the house, he would shake the walls with it. They had their private worlds, which scared me, the depth of each. I could fall in.

Allegro molto, now. The syncopation between flutes/violins and full orchestra. All the while a clarinet jig, popping up like a hand out of the deep undertones of the sea, and oh, now it isn't "Swing Low, Sweet Chariot" but something like: the symphony is filled with transformed hints of the past, keeping you longing and off balance. You are a child hoping to be tucked in and kissed before you go to sleep. The huge dark strides in, thunderous drums; then your mother comes in and quietly bends at your bed. A brief, low song, over too quickly.

This happens over and over. Full orchestra, crack of light at the door. Is this pleasant, or is it terrifying? One horn, quieter, dancing, it may be your own voice, you are trying it out, picked up by the orchestra until it's all significance, deepened, farther off, as on a meadow, coming across like wind, like storm, lightning, like armies, clashing. It's all inside you, and you are driving on, dreaming it—a little sappy, a little Spielberg.

Sometimes I ask myself why we don't rent a nice place with plumbing and heat, on a bigger, quieter lake. Some days I'm not at all nostalgic about the sacred ancestral cottage, repository of so complex a buried life. It's my father, I say, puttering around alone in the little green cottage, the one reserved for the old folks, that I mostly come back for. In spite of the past. In spite of the fact that he can't imagine we might come for his sake. "I'm paying exorbitant taxes so that all of you can have this summer resort," he says. The

three sisters look at each other, deadpan. It isn't forgiveness that we bring, exactly. It's love, I'd call it that, but the
love is a big room furnished with anger and pain.

Today is the kind of day we used to have for those edgy trips—
hazy, humid, supposed to get to ninety-five. White fences
and cornflowers getting ready to blaze with sun along the
road. I'm in here, cool, a thousand years away. Yesterday
John F. Kennedy Jr.'s plane went down. Tomorrow is the anniversary of the moon landing. I heard a replay of the space
launch, Buzz Aldrin's voice, I think, as he was looking to "a
small place where light gathers." "The earth beams," he
said. "It beckons you home." I pass Amish kids with small
bikes, riding them like scooters, right out of the fifties.

I think we've all finally given up the nostalgia for those
years that labeled them *bland* and *halcyon*. There was the
cold war, the race in space, McCarthyism, Little Rock, bomb
shelters. While my life was crashing along, music itself—
classical and popular—was crashing through to something
new, mixing genres—from Tin Pan Alley to lush ballads to
World War II dance music of big beats, rhythm and blues.
Then came Bill Haley, the DJ Alan Freed, Elvis, and the flock
that followed. These were raunchy, not bubble-gum years.
The white recording world was scared of the changes and
hated the revamping of Black songs. The Reverend John
Carroll was quoted everywhere: "Rock and Roll inflames
and excites youth like jungle tom-toms readying warriors
for battle. Inject a wrong word of misunderstanding and

the whole place blows up." I knew the Fonz in the original, as a real hood, hanging around the doorway of the school, smoking, combing his greasy hair into a careful ducktail. Dangerous, pained eyes, like my father's, someone to love and fear. My life was distributed between two counterpoised scales: aloofness and pain. One word, one look, and I lost my balance. My world exploded—imploded, rather—into marriage.

But look at me now, riding in a well-tuned fishbowl of the future, passing those Amish children. My father passed almost nobody, drove fifty miles per hour, always worried about the retread tires overheating and losing their tread, which they frequently did. All the way, he kept us alert and worrying, as if we were the Joads, down to our last dime. He had us convinced we were, and it is true, there were five of us then, Mark needing expensive drugs. We were living on an assistant professor's salary, but there were grandparents who bailed us out regularly, adding to my father's rage. On the road, we listened for a click, a bump, a faint hum. A bulge in a tire, a ping in the engine, whatever. I was too young to understand the details of possible disasters, but I knew that we were always on the edge of survival, flutes tensing up for full orchestra. Mark could have a seizure too severe to go on. He would need rest and a cool rag on his forehead. How many miles to a town?

Toward evening, we look for the cheapest motel. My father finds one on a hill up a rutted gravel road, only one small sign on the highway. We only need beds; anything else is expensive nonsense, my father says. I am looking out the screen door into fields and woods. We are in the middle of nowhere. There is no hot water. My mother says we can't stay here, and cries a little about Mark's having diarrhea and needing a bath, about needing a bath herself, about the dinginess of the towels and bedspreads.

Did we actually stay there? I only remember the tears, the tension. And the next morning's rain. The only place we can find for breakfast is a nice, white-tablecloth restaurant with real butter in separate pats on the plate, and real cream for the oatmeal, making it luxuriously slick. The large windows, dark with rain; my father's face, dark with anger; the waiter, the white bowls. The room appears to me all white, like Daisy Buchanan's parlor, and my father is the terrible storm, trees throwing limbs down in the road.

The tire starts to thump, then the flap-flap of the retread coming off. We count the miles riding on the spare. How long can it hold up? Then we sit in the heat outside Valparaiso, Indiana, while the tire is being changed; we have a Coke, or a drink of milk from one of the twin Scotch thermoses in the zippered lunch kit with the tin sandwich box. From the gas station radio, Mitch Miller's "The Yellow Rose of Texas" and Johnny Desmond's "Love Is a Many Splendored Thing," or so I imagine, now, as those songs rise in me, called up somehow by this scene. These songs came early, poised just before the edge of Rock & Roll. In 1956, Fats Domino crossed the charts with "Blueberry Hill," and Elvis Presley recorded Carl Perkins's "Blue Suede Shoes." *Teen-ager* was a new catchword, and I was twelve, on the edge of my life. Back on the road, my mother rolls up the side window, pinning an undershirt there against the sun. For a little while, life feels cool and comfortable.

Largo

In my present life, it's barely eight in the morning, still cool. The Susquehanna River's luminescent in the sun. This is the part of the music that picks up the one simple phrase, "Going home," from the old spiritual, floating like a ghost across the fields, rising, echoing itself. Horns turn the meandering thought into a pronouncement: going to that other world hidden within this one like the quiet, green rivers between the lakes, the one hidden in my heart, where we are canoeing all day up the Chain of Lakes, through lily pads and rushes. At Ellsworth, we paddle so close to the road we can see cars, hear a car radio playing the "Banana Boat Song" by Harry Belafonte, or something else incongruous that makes it clear how hard it is to stay in the other world.

Now the phrase returns, "Going home," in a more adult voice, filling out. Orchestra rising. Of course it's sad, going home, with all that's gone and all that comes back in your mind, but when you turn your eyes that way, the whole of this present life stands in relief against it. Neither would exist but for the other. Now we're doing the last hard paddling before the town dock, blessedly helped along by the winds. My father's doing most of the work, as usual, and singing. He's happy as a child. Now even the cello in the background is on the move, bringing along a following of sleepy, stringed voices, slowly on their way.

In my memory's slow journey to the lake, there is lunch under one tree, the sun very hot. We can't find a picnic table, so we stop at the edge of a cornfield, and when we let Margaret the cat out to pee, she slips off her homemade leash. Would my father let us buy a real one? No. I'm running down the rows of corn, calling, furious at something, at whoever let the cat go, at the hot, infuriating world where cats have to wear leashes, at Mark, sweating and having his oversized diaper changed on a blanket where every passing car could see. Millie remembers that I was mad because we were made to sit apart from each other in the grass, to stop our fighting. She says I yelled, "I'm going to get poison ivy!" All I remember is anger, and hiding in the corn, letting them call for me a while. I come out covered with dust and husks; so does the cat. Once I think we even took a litter of kittens along. I think I see them in a box in the back seat because my father wouldn't pay someone to take care of them at home. But the picture's fuzzy, everything subsumed by the dominant theme, Lost Cat in the Cornfield.

Oh yes, now comes the voice of experience: Life Is Like That. A combined sadness and joy in the music here, a released breath. Then the flutes, a village dance. Horns, announcing the dance. Everything is here, the heart is a village square. Look around. Nothing has been overlooked. Sisters are wrestling and playing Ouncie-the-dog, a drama they make up in their cramped back seat; retarded brothers are falling forward, their muscles tensed in seizures. Mothers are trying to get pills down their throats. Fathers are chewing on their tongues, listening for the faint whine of disaster. The one horn speaks for all. It is going home, has gone, will go, and it is willing now to be quiet. The strings pick up, just to keep the melody, not let it die. I think this is their only goal. It's so pretty, just keep it, hum it, so long as breath lasts. Then the whole orchestra lets out its voice. Low, horns, across a huge, wide valley, with no bottom. One last low breath.

Horns. How many repetitions of the theme are still possible? Where I am now is noisy, road work going on everywhere, the current federal budget surplus a bonanza for Interstate highway contractors. Money thrown around like crazy, my father says. Orange-and-white-striped canisters line the road like Dr. Seuss hats. Near Harrisburg, there are four-foot concrete barriers on both sides of me. I'm a race car driver in a tunnel, but when I can look across the distance again, the hills of Western Pennsylvania roll softly, like the Ozarks, bluish in the heat-haze. I'm stopped for a few minutes by the construction. Beside me is a truck from New

York with orange crates of chickens. I can see only flickers of feathers. I turn off the air conditioning and open my windows. Now I see their doomed, flickering wattles. It seems odd for chickens to be from New York. I greet them silently, a native of Arkansas chicken country, and of the soft Ozark hills. So many pieces of my life are meeting up lately, as if I were at a class reunion.

You tell yourself the story of your life as you live it. You invest it with themes, with significance. You raise certain parts up, you use those as symbols of the parts you've lost forever. A hammer falls from the sailboat into the lake. There is my tanned father on his knees by the cedar trees, arms outstretched in a bow before his father, crying out in mock submission, "Oh Father, I have dropped the hammer in the lake. I am a worthless worm, not worthy of your forgiveness." I see Grandfather's wry smile. He's leaning on his good leg, at a critical slant to the world. We are all giggling children. This scene stands for my father, I might say, for my version of the truth under the joke—his real fear of his domineering father, his sublimated anger, his childish joy.

But there are other variations, each separate but fluid, as if a child's eyes were turning first here, then there, picking up colors and shapes. My brother falls from the sailboat into the lake. My father dives for him, catching his ankle on a rope as he goes over the side. My mother and grandmother have been sitting on the dock talking. Millie and I are wading, looking for mussels. We all look up, speechless. For a

moment, both father and son are doomed, sails flapping
out of control, sliders rattling in the wind. I don't know what
I want to happen, what I feel, what solution would make
the world better for us all. Then with perfect strength, my
father pulls himself up by his ankle, holding my brother.
Two drenched wrestlers collapse on the lurching deck. Finally, Mark is riding ashore on my father's shoulders, pur-
ple-lipped, babbling and smiling. This scene, saved out of
time and out of context, stands for my ambivalence, my
fuzzy hold on what might have been the truth.

It's good to look around, to see that some things are settled facts. In 1956, Dwight Eisenhower went to Walter Reed
Hospital because of an abdominal obstruction, my sixth
grade class went across the hall to watch Grace Kelly get
married on TV, Soviet troops went to Poland and Hungary
to suppress revolts, and the Italian luxury liner, the *Andrea
Doria*, sank. Floyd Patterson became the youngest world
champion in boxing; Tommy Dorsey choked to death in his
sleep. The first black woman enrolled at the University of
Alabama, backed by court order and bayonets. It's good
to have headlines that nurture you with their bold decla-
rations of truth.

Scherzo
Bang, slam, the Scherzo starts off with the father who has
lost a bottle of glue, who rages through the cottage all night

long in only his boxer shorts, raising bedcovers, overturning boxes, throwing down the contents of closet shelves, rifling through newspapers, on his knees irrationally digging through the stored junk in the "secret" compartment of the attic, terrified of loss, terrifying. Something's loose in the universe, closing in. My mother's white-faced, mute, waiting it out, lying across the bed in the lamplight. My father's ranting, "I don't deserve to live if I'm so stupid I can't hang onto one miserable bottle of glue." We sense that this is not hyperbole to him. He has held us hostage to his suicide threats before, like a child who says I'll hold my breath till I die, but also like an adult who could actually find a way to do it.

Here they are now, the flutes, hiding like children, but okay. This is what happens. Things pick up. It's the whole orchestra, not the old melody. This one rising, inquisitive. Raising its eyebrows. A little nervous on clarinet and strings. Things are speeding up, looking around, figuring out how to live.

How to live. Go along. Say nothing. Millie and I are playing flashlight tag now, because we have to or be teased and tormented by Richie, Alan, and Tom. We are supposed to be looking, but are mostly hiding from them. They slip out of their secret places; they make wild noises in the dark. No place is safe. The light draws them. The woods are a well-established pattern of trails and nests. We move from one to the other. We have to shine our nervous light if we want to play.

And so strings and horns come up with a dance. The clarinet begins as a single voice, and the orchestra runs back over the range of possibilities before it comes up with the simplest version, a note struck twice, rising step by step, then quickly descending, a tire with the air let out. The heat has melted the tread off, and we are sitting in the car outside a farmhouse. My father is standing at the screen door, whistling instead of knocking, as if he doesn't want to disturb the universe. As if he's afraid to exist, as if we don't exist. The falling note feels strangely beautiful. I am only partially involved, watching myself fall, slow motion, off the end of the world. Maybe I don't exist. Maybe no one can see me. A deep, hot flush of fear.

Then four low notes, four higher, climbing up to where the orchestra takes over. I'm not alone. I'm at the gas station, drawing cold circles on Millie's arm with a bottle of Grapette, until my worry goes to sleep and my heart is able to move freely. Flutes above, drums below—it could be worse, it could be better. They go on dancing; it's a different sound now, embellished. They do this until the long shiver of strings, the annunciation of the horns. Here my favorite phrase comes back, full of itself, and escapes before it's over, as if someone forgot to finish it. The strings make the softest holding. Then silence. Then one hard jolt.

If the summer of 1956 is the end of my childhood, it is only later that I see that.

That fall, Elvis Presley appeared on the Ed Sullivan show. I watched because I was supposed to want to, and because my father scorned him, but I wasn't very interested yet. I bought records like Tab Hunter's "Young Love" before Elvis's darkness began to draw me. By the next summer, the lake for me was a hunting ground of another sort. Then I didn't go back for years, absorbed as I was in pulling away, in finding out, year by year, that I wasn't at all away.

After Dvořák, I still have nine hours ahead of me before I stop. I listen to my Elvis tapes, Horowitz, Carmen Fantasy for Violin, Roy Orbison, Emmy Lou, and on the radio, the news, Dr. Laura dispensing morality and hawking her book, *Ten Stupid Things Women Do to Mess Up Their Lives*, and a violin quartet version of "Finlandia," wistful, as if the Nazis never existed. Sometimes when the signal starts sputtering, I ride in silence. The Pennsylvania Turnpike simply turns into the Ohio Turnpike, then straight north on 27 just past Toledo, those three giant steps. It's wonderful to be able to drive sixty-five and seventy miles an hour most of the way.

Allegro
It feels over, then, the way a symphony does, the way Dvořák's symphony brings back the melody again: strident, purposeful, transformed into ritual. *The arrival*: my father comes up the hill to meet me, a little bent, thinner, sinewy and dark

as an old piece of leather, his steel-gray hair neatly slicked back in anticipation of my arrival. We hug. We rub each other's backs, awkwardly, the way people do who can never say what they mean. He's been hanging out the wash. He starts reciting what groceries he has, that we're welcome to, what we might need to get. He offers to go, but I turn him down, knowing all the things I'll buy that he wouldn't approve of. *The gathering:* My sisters arrive. A great wallowing of quilts and clothing, a cloud of cleaning. Water's pumped. The wooden bucket's left outside full of water, to swell so that it won't leak. Vegetables are chopped. *The chorus:* Three grown-up sisters are sitting in a row on the narrow old dock under a nearly-full moon so bright only the Big Dipper's visible. It's late. Light's out in the little green cottage where our father sleeps. Now most of the lights along the lake have gone out. The moon's reflection travels the length of the water, directly to us. Our father's sailboat's resolutely anchored—maybe for the last year—where it's always been, about twenty feet out and to the north, toward town. "If I didn't have to make money, I'd build a boat and sail around the world. I'd stay on the boat forever," he used to say. "What's the good of a house? You can't sail it." He's eighty-two. He spent this last winter making new sails.

Our mother, our brother, and all the other ghosts barely shimmer, not needing to go anywhere. It is so fluty and beautiful out here we can hardly stand it. "How beautiful!" we sisters say, because there is nothing else to do about it. We drink two bottles of wine between eleven and two o'clock.

Echoes of "Three Blind Mice" at this point in the music.
Not blind, exactly. I've married and divorced two versions
of my father, and then done my time in therapy. Millie and
Michelle are both figuring out what to do with their anxiety. You don't want to blind yourself, but it's good to ease
up at last, if you can, to celebrate the pinpoint of time that
belongs to you, among the centuries, to bring all of time
to bear on it: the music, the art, the drama. To laugh. "But
soft!" Millie says. "What light across yonder lake doth break?
It is the moon. The sun doth percheth on the other side, in
China." "Ah yes," I reply. "Yonder stars fixeth themselves, so
we can tell where we are, so we won't falleth off the dock."
The French horn triumphs not by will, but by energy. And
still, the oboe wants to come back, and the Three-Blind-
Mice strings. Every sweet phrase a person could hope for
returns and takes a bow. When my favorite one comes, it
stands up, bends softly, and stretches; then, its shadow is
lifted up loud and dramatic across the water, and turned to
each side as if it were an Oscar on a pedestal: an artifact.
You present your life to yourself. You give it a happier ending, make a shapeliness out of it. Then art sends you back
to memory, where it came from. You can't have the original,
which maybe never was the right thing, but you can have
this. And soft, the little wisps, rising from the lake: the angels, the annunciation. You have to bow your head, to re-
ceive it, all of it, down on you, its sheer trumpets, clarinets,
the joy of its French horns.

Walls Six Feet Thick

I climb down from his bed made of railroad ties, which time can never destroy. At least, every time I remember it, it's in the present tense. There's a .44 on one bedpost, a huge glass ashtray full of Marlboro butts on another. The sunlight's no match for the red curtains, which give the room the feel of a tavern in early morning: awkward, waiting for dark. I wrap his flannel shirt over my bare skin—compared to my ex-husband's shirts, it's spacious as a bathrobe. I step quickly down the cold hallway to the shower. The house feels half-constructed, no baseboards, no paint in the hallway, the kitchen countertop raw plywood. The previous owner apparently quit on the house and sold it to Roy, who has built a deck but otherwise made no effort toward finish work. It's drafty, too, which is good, because the drafts waft away some of the animal smell. Roy's already up, outside throwing last night's steak bones to Luke and Jack. I can hear him affectionately slapping the sides of their heads so hard they yelp, driving them away to watch them return, asking for more pain. Even back then, I keep as far away as an anthropologist, picturing the interdependence of man and dog.

The bathroom carpet's damp and musty, the cut-to-fit kind, orange shag, jammed up against the shower stall. The floor of the shower is slimy, but water's water, I think, squeezing Prell so old it thickly bulges its way out of the bottle. Light filters through the filthy window. I'm humming "Longfellow Serenade," which was playing when I fell asleep. It's not Henry Wadsworth in the song. "Come on baby, ride," kept going on into my sleep, blending Neil Diamond into my dreams, and—stretching the imagination—Roy into Neil Diamond, one vague sexual fluidity.

After my shower, I am shivering in my skirt and blouse. I'm thin, and it's cold in the house. He keeps it cold, being heavy himself—short, top-heavy and dense, like a wrestler. Sometimes we sleep tangled together on the sagging sofa in front of the fireplace, where he builds a massive fire. Then when I wake, I am stiff and hot, but feeling held, enclosed, exactly safe enough to have stayed the night.

He's made coffee and eggs and bacon, clearing a spot on the table in the sunlight for my plate and cup, trying for delicacy. He lights a cigarette, takes a few drags through his muddy-blonde Kung-fu moustache and grinds it out. "I punched the bag already," he tells me, "twenty minutes. Before you got up." He smiles, pleased as a kid, feeling slim, sliding four eggs onto his plate to make up for it. His smile,

as usual, is a half leer, to show he isn't taking himself seriously, that maybe nothing is serious here, that maybe nothing will last, but who can be sure?

"Good for you," I say, smiling. It is my long habit of bol-
stering my man, independent of circumstances. Nothing
has anything to do with anything, for now. I am drinking
coffee in sunlight.

The long road down the mountain is full of ruts that the
low Buick Skylark—my ex's choice—does not like, but I've
learned to maneuver around the worst of them. Roy's brown
ranch house is almost at the upper end of the road, in an
open field studded with tiny pine trees he got from the Arkansas State Department of Agriculture. Beyond his land, in
the big trees, is one other house: dark, and full of pale, ret-
icent children and assorted fat adults. Cars sit on concrete
blocks up here, sofas collapse on porches. It takes twenty
minutes to get from this point east of West Fork to Fayetteville, ten of those just to get down off the mountain. I know.
I've timed it for months. One time my car got stuck in the
mud, and I hitched a ride up the hill with a man in a pickup,
two rifles on his rack behind us. Who would have thought I
would take such chances? I recognize that something in me
is desperate, crazy. I study myself, astonished.

There's a lot to study. Today, for instance, I go straight from
his house to the First Christian Church. In the twenty-min-
ute drive, I rehearse the prayer I've written. I pray it aloud,

getting the tone right, but really praying it, too. I like writing prayers, one of the best things about being an elder, the first woman elder in the church, and at the age of thirty, the youngest. Elders are spiritual leaders, elected by the deacons. You get to stand behind the communion table under the dark oak arch filled with organ pipes, and hand the brass trays to the deacons. From that spot, surrounded by old wood, you can look straight back at the stained-glass picture of Jesus walking on water. I have often thought the congregation ought to get to face those windows, instead of the pipes and the cross. In the long years before I finally had the courage to get a divorce, I depended on the church for art, music, and philosophy. I took free courses in theology at the Presbyterian Campus Center. During a year or so of pastoral counseling, I fell in love with the minister, I fell in love with Abstract Love and determined to have it, to be it, to merge with its aesthetic. I was trying to learn to be a good poet. For practice, I wrote prayers to make you weep, to occasionally raise the hairs on the back of your neck. I revised and revised. Each week, I read the scripture and based my prayer on that. Like a good poem, each prayer in its meticulous stages of shaping came closer and closer to an utter sincerity. Sometimes when I was standing at the lectern, Mark at the pulpit across from me, each of us in our black robes, I felt as ordained as he. I felt as if we were a couple, united by a complex love for the abstract that few others would be able to comprehend—a passionate, yet unconsummated love, a holy longing.

Separate scenes, still electric, still in progress, are suspended inside all my attempts to understand them. I don the weighty robe, still feeling Roy's tongue in my mouth. I think of that word, *don*, which just came up in the graduate linguistics course I'm taking at night: the combination of *do* and *on*, "to envelop oneself in, to assume." Beside me in the sacristy, the women are filling the tiny glass communion cups with Welch's grape juice—Doris Bently, Mary Lou Wheatley, and Sara Gifford. They are wearing flowered aprons. Enveloped by faithfulness, I smile and say hello. I am a minister, looking after my flock. I love them all. They have saved me from emptiness, they have clasped their arms together to catch me and my children when I fell out of my marriage. I have won them for myself. For a second, I have a vision of my ex, wedging in beside me, late, in a back pew last Christmas Eve, reeking of Jack Daniels. Now, he never shows up. When I process down the right aisle to the front of the church, Mark down the left aisle, I am collecting in my mind individual souls, one row at a time, filling my heart, giving out what I can muster. I offer them what I have, a little of the flush of last night, keeping most of it for myself.

Driving back up the mountain after church, though, I begin to tighten, thinking of the school week ahead, papers to grade, the grocery store, the kids' lunches, having to face their father as he delivers the kids to what used to be his own back door, his face glowering and closed. I mentally close the door on him. I make the last curve to Roy's house, resolutely free. He is lining up water-filled gallon milk jugs on the fence posts. "How about a little target shooting?" he asks. "Want to go first?" He hands me the ear plugs and the heavy .44. This is the part I like least, particularly the noise, which rings in my ears, in spite of the plugs, forever after. But I'm not chicken. I hold the gun, left hand steadying my right, both eyes open, looking just over the top of the sight. I squeeze the trigger slowly, so as not to disturb the position of the barrel. I relax my arm to avoid the pain of the kickback. It gets me. Not as bad as it does with the rifles, but my arm pitches backward into my shoulder. The loud report, the sharp jolt, makes me feel out of control, in the hands of a terrible fate. The jug completely disappears.

"Did you *know*," he begins, index finger in the air, leering, preparing to fire a piece of information like a bullet at the ignorance of the world, "that the M16 rifle can penetrate a steel helmet at five hundred meters?"

The first time I came here, it was midsummer. It was only a few weeks after my divorce was final. On a Monday I had taken the kids to swim in the White River, a spot with a small waterfall, where there used to be a mill. I was lying on the bank. Roy was on the other side, watching teenagers swing out and jump from a knotted rope into the deepest pool. He floated calculatedly as an alligator up beside the rock where I was lying. I saw everything about him at once, what it all meant—his drooping moustache, red face, staged smile, acne scars, heavy belly and shoulders, short legs. Or I didn't. I don't know. He sensed my loneliness as if I were broadcasting it in concentric circles into the water. He knew I was desperate enough to agree to go out with him. I have to say, though, there is more to it than that. I have always been drawn to the kind of person who lurks on the fringes, the kind of ugly ones who would think I am a fairy princess. My ex was no Paul Newman, that's for sure. I was pretty: classic nose, big brown eyes—if you could've seen them under my glasses—and a good figure. But I always felt that inside me lived a troll: wizened, rejected, one eye cocked at the world. In high school, like most girls, I wanted desperately to be a cheerleader. I had all the qualities—I was athletic, pretty, spirited—but when I tried out, the troll snickered in my ear, slowing my reaction time. I couldn't believe in myself, jumping up and down and waving pompoms.

I wasn't surprised when Roy picked me up on Friday in a real army-type Jeep and said he'd decided to cook at his house, if that was all right with me. "Listen, you don't have to do anything you don't want to do," he said, and I understood him perfectly, knowing exactly what I would do. He threw huge steaks on the grill. "I can't eat that much!" I protested. "Oh shucks," he replied, leering, doing his redneck imitation. "The dogs will be so sad." Steak, bread, and wine. That was it. And then we took wine down to the pond and sat on a rickety section of dock and watched the frogs.

"After dark vapours have oppressed our plains
For a long dreary season, comes a day
Born of the gentle South, and clears away
From the sick heavens all unseemly stains,"

he recited like a teacher, in a rich radio voice. "Keats," he said. "'Sleep and Poetry.' I have some pitiful offerings of my own, a couple of which I shall say for you, if I may." Chin up, he peered over the top of his ragged moustache, and began. His poems came off better aloud than on paper, but they weren't bad. After all those years of being married to an engineer, I was glad to hear any kind of poem, sincerely spoken. When I try to remember them now, all I can hear is Neil Diamond. Roy might as well have been doing "Long-fellow Serenade": "Sing, sing my song, let me sing my song / let me make it warm for you."

His history lay all around me, it turns out. When I was eleven, I was sewing doll clothes and stuck a needle in the rug, forgot about it and crawled across it. We had just moved to town and knew no doctors. My father picked Roy's father, old Dr. Hackett, from the phone book. Bushy-haired and cold-eyed, he attacked my knee, dug the broken-off needle out of my bone, making a horrible scar. "Quit your belly-aching," I remember his tone. "You're not going to die of it."

And then, wonder of all wonders, Roy's uncle Hackett had been the judge at my divorce. "Why do you want this divorce?" he had asked, even though my lawyer had assured me I would only have to answer easy questions relating to the children. Suddenly, I was on trial for my life, stumbling over years of misery to find one answer that would satisfy him. "He made me feel bad," I replied idiotically.

In a town with only one high school and junior high, Roy and I—never meeting—had gone to the same schools, he a couple of years behind me, as well as to the local university, but there our parallel paths diverged with a vengeance. I had kids; he went to Vietnam. A sniper, he had killed any number of people, including women. Maybe children, but he wouldn't say. The war was still going on in his brain. He approached the small creatures of this world as if he could decide at any minute to end their lives, as if he were giving them a gift, for now, by not doing so.

He could rescind the gift. Queen had been snarling and roaming too far, he said. The neighbors had complained. When I arrived one weekend, he told me he'd shot her and buried her out back. "I hated it," he mused, stroking down to the tips of his mustache, "but she might have hurt someone. I did a good job, one clean bullet and she dropped like a sack of potatoes. I should have shot her where I was going to bury her, though. I had a time moving her, and got blood all over everything," he said, tilting his head toward the still-bloody sink, the blood-soaked rags on the counter. "This is what it comes down to," I thought, "flesh and blood." All my senses heightened, for good and for ill, for a while.

At least five cats draped themselves across the sofa and chairs. He would slap them the way he did the dogs, only not so hard. Sometimes he would send them flying across the room into a wall. He was never angry when he did this. He would as soon pick them up and cradle them in his arms as slap them. It was as if he had to keep testing to see what the limits of life are, to trust it, to see how much you can do to it and it will still go on. He brought his muscular arm down in huge sweeps, but as graceful as a ballet dancer. There was no point in anything less, in the vast universe he lived in. It was the universe of his favorite movie, 2001: A Space Odyssey. The small, ordinary world cringed.

The enemy could show up at any time. Over the rise, up from the pond, they would come, with their automatic rifles. They would be wearing masks and would ram down the door. They would run their tanks over every unfortified wall. There was still time to get ready, maybe, but one could not be too alert. There would be the dogs to begin with, then the .44 on the bedpost and the rifles in the adjoining room. He unrolled exact architectural drawings of the house as it would look when he got the six-foot-thick stone walls built. The interior would be scrolled like a nautilus shell inward, to the safe center, with guns and a month's supply of food. He worried some about how he would get the stubborn cats into the center quickly enough.

Guns and food and books. Roy had built what looked like a real library, with freestanding stacks, in one of the bedrooms. "Did you *know* that Spinoza, not Descartes, is responsible for ending medieval philosophy?"

"Okay, why?" I am dragged into this.

"Because Spinoza, unlike Descartes, denied the possibility of harmonizing reason with Biblical revelation. He said man has to attain knowledge of his union with the whole of nature, to attain eternal bliss. You can see how this would collapse all previous philosophies." He had two long shelves of philosophy, four of history, five of classical literature, and a whole section devoted to poetry. A few contemporary novels were piled in the corners, but it was the dark, musty ones with faintly gilt titles, that he liked best. He would read long passages aloud to me, stretched out on the bed, running his hand over my hair.

When I met him, he was teaching in a summer program for delinquent kids. Those were the teenagers at the White River. The next fall, I convinced my principal at Sherwood High School to hire him. "I take your recommendation seriously," he said, frowning, uneasy with his decision. So for the next school year, until he got fired for allegedly writing suggestive comments in his students' journals, Roy and I were colleagues. His room was next to mine. He would swagger into 204 and ceremoniously drop a folded note on my desk, clearing his throat. "This is an agenda for the meeting," he would say, looking dispassionately out across the heads of the students. I would not read it right away, not being able to keep as straight a face. Sometimes I would watch him coming my way, down the lower hall, a cave man in a tie. "What have I done?" I would ask myself in some part of my brain that didn't bother to answer. Fridays, though, I would be singing inside, all day. I had never counted hours, but now I was like my students, wild to get free, to get the kids off to their dad's, to hear the Jeep in the driveway, to head out, away from civilization.

These were the early seventies. I pretty much missed the sixties. While Fayetteville churned with antiwar protests and flower children, I was having babies, washing and folding diapers, missing my youth, feeling outraged deep in my soul. It was a wonderful time to be outraged. On Dickson street at George's Lounge, you could get professional anti-draft counseling twenty-four hours a day. Several graduate students were rumored to have been involved in setting off bombs in the restroom of the Capitol building in Washington, and the word went out: "Feds are everywhere, looking for clues." A group of creative writing faculty climbed the giant pine tree in front of the student union, nude, to protest the war. I can't remember their reasoning, but what mattered was the nakedness, however stylized, of body and spirit. An "underground" paper, The Grapevine, started up by hippies and graduate students, ran poems about marijuana and free love, caricatures of Nixon-the-antichrist, as well as great movie reviews and editorials. A lot of the local writers—Barry Hannah, Frank Stanford, Leon Stokesbury, Jack Butler, and others—went on to be well-known novelists and poets. On street corners, students piled up and gave away all their worldly possessions, to demonstrate to the world the blessings of communal living. I longed to be in the middle of it all, wearing round glasses, long, straight hair, and a paisley sarong. I did get the round glasses, but I quit wearing them because my husband hated them, knowing they stood for something in me he could never satisfy. I would drift into one of the head shops along Dickson Street and inhale the incense of an alternate life.

By the time the idealism of the midsixties had given way to the horrors of Kent State and the first news of Watergate, I was teaching high school. The accumulated rage against the war, against Nixon, against America's imperialist aggression, drove itself down, now, into acid rock, into harder drugs. I didn't care. It was all I could do to hang on, day after day, grading papers, fending off the cataclysmic end of my marriage a while longer. Hippies had their LSD; like Mrs. Robinson in *The Graduate*, I tried valium. Only a few, to take the edge off, but one Sunday I sat in the back yard in my bathrobe and held the bottle in my fist all morning, thinking I would swallow them all. The sun was shining, the sky was a piercing Arkansas blue. I hardly knew where I was. While I still had the energy, I got up and went inside. When the entire thirty pills circled and flushed down the toilet, my marriage was over.

Roy had never smoked marijuana, but he didn't like to admit it. I had only tried it once or twice. Roy's ex-graduate-student-hippie friend, Ned, brought us some and urged us to give it a try. No one who has ever gotten high can forget the strange sense that, while it seems nothing is changed—objects sit where they always have, people say the same things—the world turns out to be easier, gentler, slower, brighter, than you thought it was. And when you wake in the morning, there's no hangover, nothing's left except a knowledge that feels as if it's trapped in amber. If you could get to it . . . Still, we finished the joints Ned left us and made no attempt to get more. As much as Roy longed to be a hippie, his soul disapproved. Survival required clear-headed vigilance.

Once there was a woman peeing in the rice paddies. She squatted, her loose gray trousers spread as far as possible at her ankles. She was holding the bottoms of her trousers to keep them away from her muddy feet. Her long hair was falling out of its knot, down her back. Her head tilted upward, alert as a deer. Through the trees, a man knelt on one knee to steady his rifle. Her bare buttocks would have made an easy target, but she might have survived. He aimed just to the left of her spine, careful to leave a clear path for the bullet to reach her heart.

"They were all in on it," he said. "You couldn't assume anything. You'd leave one old woman alone, out of sympathy, and next thing you know, gooks would be falling out of the trees on your whole platoon. She would have heard you, and told them. Ever put your buddy's arm in a bag, not knowing if you got the right arm with the right body?"

I rewind my present-tense memory a little way back, before the shooting, to get hold of myself. I am singing "Come Thou Fount of Every Blessing" all the way back from church, trying to fend off the beginning of the school week. I always get started on songs, like a mantra. I believe that somewhere deep inside, I can sing really well, but I just don't know how to do it on the surface. Maybe the troll can sing, I don't know. Once I tried to join the choir, because the choirmaster seemed so desperate for new members. "What are you singing, alto or soprano?" he asked, leaning down right at my mouth, trying to figure out if I was singing at all. I keep trying to teach myself. There is that point at which the voice has to shift to a higher register, for instance in the third line, "Prone to wander, Lord I feel it, Prone to leave the God I love," is a huge jump upward from the previous two lines. I can't do them without going into a kind of trill which is clearly not my natural voice. I guess I should be an alto, but I don't know how to harmonize. Anyway, I get to the last lines, "Praise the mount! I'm fixed upon it, Mount of Thy Redeeming Love," and my voice goes all over the place. I'm wondering how anyone can sing this song without grinning. Now I feel better. I am singing it all the way up the mount.

After the guns, we go inside. Roy has been cleaning house, which means he has scooped up a few of the old cat piles in the corner of the living room and has dumped a layer of new litter in the various pans. He has washed some dishes and is grading papers. I have brought my own papers to grade. I notice that we have settled into a domesticity more frightening to me than the guns.

I have heard that if you use one of those white-noise machines to sleep by long enough, you get to be deaf to those particular tones. It is like that with most things. It is not so much that you settle for what you have. What you have just gets to be normal, and after a while, normal seems good because you can predict it. Then after a longer while, you think something is good just *because* it is normal. Finally, good isn't an issue any more. Your life just is. I know. I watch Roy sitting across from me with his coffee and cigarette, raising one pale eyebrow over some idiotic thing a student has written. I guess we're all lovable if you could keep each of our tiny aspects suspended, unanchored in time, but you can't. I know I have to get out of here, soon.

"Let's take a hike down the creek," I say, which is as far as I can get, at the moment, toward that end.

It's November, and the trees are bare. We angle down the hill, past the pond and onto God-knows-whose property. The creek bed looks like a moonscape, almost completely dry gravel at the bottom and huge boulders halfway up the hill on either side. I have on sneakers, not so good for this. Roy has on his Army boots, real ones, from back then. He reaches for me, lifting me across the gaps. I resist being lifted, looked after.

I do like Roy best outside, chopping wood or following a dry creek bed. There, I don't have to try to fit him in with anything. I don't have to have the kids around him. I don't have to introduce him to my friends. I would like to keep him here, in his fortress, and drive out when I feel like it. It occurs to me that men have had this plan for centuries.

I follow his back, his camouflage jacket. I suddenly feel a great tenderness for his back, almost love, knowing the future's broad outlines, if not its details. By next month, all this will be history. There are things you know, what's deep inside you, like a song, that is still working to find out what to do at the tangible level of the vocal cords, the mouth and tongue. You say all sorts of things, you kiss slobbery or hard-lipped, working on it. This life or next, it's going to find its way.

It could be the shoes, not enough support. I twist my ankle, bad, on the rocks. He turns at once, hearing my "Oh!" I am splayed awkwardly across two uneven rocks, hands gripping the small bushes on either side. He steps carefully between my arms and over my chest. "Don't move," he commands. He kneels and lifts my foot as if it were a newborn baby, supporting it on all sides with his hands. Gently, he pushes at one spot with his thumb. "Does that hurt?" he asks. "Here? Okay, how about here? Uh, huh," he says to himself, like a doctor. When he touches the worst of it, I try not to cry, but a tear, more than one, rolls down from my right eye. I wipe my face, pretending it's the cold. "Do you think you can stand on the other foot?" he asks. He lifts me up, sparing me the trouble. He wedges his shoulder under mine, using it as a crutch for me to lean on. "Now, just take one careful hop," he insists. I do it, letting out a hard breath. "Now, one more," he says, straining to hold me upright.

We stay in the smoother creek bottom as long as we can. To get back up the steep rocks, he has me sit down and scoot upward, using only my hands, as he pulls me by the shoulders, little by little. He gives commands clearly, exactly, telling me where to put my good foot, where to rest the other one, on each upward pull. Sometimes I have to stop and clench against the pain for a minute. It is strangely delicious—real, physical, isolating. I barely notice and no longer care that off and on I let out childlike sobs. At the top of the hill, at the far edge of his field, he orders, "Don't try to come any farther. I'll be back in a few minutes."

After a while, the deep thrum of his riding mower breaks through my private preoccupation with the expanding and contracting of pain. He has brought a blanket, and he lifts me carefully onto his lap, wrapping it around my legs. At the end of this scene that I have stored forever, we are riding together over the bumpy field into the late afternoon light, his arms reaching around me on both sides to steer, smashing his precious new pine trees left and right.

Summer House

Here we are, in a rented house at the Cape again. When you're a mother and grandmother, you go where your children go, if they ask you along. It's nice here, but my ideal is still our Central Lake cottage—only larger and with running water, I suppose. To appreciate it best, you'd need to spend three hot days on the road, the way we used to. Then you'd be under the trees at last, smelling lake. You'd smell the back porch before you get to it. It would actually be the inside coming out, a whole winter of closed-up cedar, of must and dust. Even now I smell it: low, rich, like a galvanized bucket full of water and sand. It's dark inside, in the little kitchen, but beyond it is the screened-in porch, the lake glinting like foil off its ceiling, off the oiled tablecloth. To the left of the kitchen is the small dining room with the stairs to the loft. Between the dining room and the living room is the brick fireplace, warming both sides. The fireplace is old, small and unassuming. All I have ever wanted is a cedar room and a fireplace of old bricks. That's not much to ask, I have said a number of times.

A summer house is like a perfect mother, in a way. You can't live in it all your life, but it lives in you. You think about it in December, how the snow must look. It rests easy there; it lets you go when you must. There are other places like this—the tent my first husband and I used, that smelled of canvas, not nylon—rich, waxy—its ropes that tried to proclaim with every breeze their dedication to permanence. And before that, the plastic sheets we threw over our quilts by the White River, where we slept with no gear at all, boiling coffee and pouring off the top to avoid the grounds. I remember these times with great joy, the way we nurtured ourselves, taking care of the details of living with mindfulness for a change, enclosed in the chores of staying alive.

When you pare down, every action, every utensil and piece of furniture carries greater significance, like a poem. It feels as though each object grows in the imagination like a mushroom, its edges lapping over until much of its story is tucked underneath, out of sight. Everything's potential, like the first sounds and shapes a baby notices.

A cottage is a cool shadow, holding what it holds under a great space of sky. To our grandson Josh, each one is his "beach house." The one we're in now has a wraparound porch, part of it enclosed, which keeps Noah, the youngest, from crawling off the edge. Josh can remember the one in Harwichport, across the main street and three blocks from the ocean, but he can't remember the first one, the tiny little upstairs apartment just across the dunes from the beach. That summer he was twenty months old, Zach was a baby in an infant seat, and Noah was four years away. We were crowded in, unable to pass each other on the dark, narrow stairway. Cape Cod cottages are often fortified with wood paneling—even on staircases—against the Atlantic bluster, but they feel hot and stuffy in August. Rental houses have artificial flowers, and pictures painted by local artists. This latest one, down the road from Harwichport in the more elegant village of Chatham, has three portraits painted by someone named Wendell Rogers. We try to imagine the names of his subjects, the women uprightly pretty—wife, or sister, and daughter of a businessman. We decide his profession by his face. Impressed with the seriousness of portraiture, his lips are upturned only at the edges. We name him Willard. Above the fireplace is a painting of a rowboat stranded far up on a wide expanse of sand. The tide has no doubt gone out. The fireplace has a large piece of Plexiglas over the opening, a basket of multicolored dried flowers inside, and a sign overhead that says, "Do not use," in case you might feel like removing the dozen or so screws in the Plexiglas.

Four bedrooms are under the open rafters, nice for sleeping on a rainy night, but the sound carries from one room to the next over the tops of the walls, which are basically partitions. Of the various vacation cottages Kelly and Doron have rented, this one is the most like Central Lake: lots of cedar rooms, and you live on top of each other, unable to get any privacy. The upstairs shower is useless, made up of a pipe raised over an old-fashioned claw-foot bathtub. The water comes out all hot or all cold. But the view is amazing, like on a postcard, the house on a cliff with a long stretch of marsh directly below. You can look out the windows on three sides and see water. Every night, we get a tacky expanse of sunset over the sea, with sailboats. It would be perfect if it weren't for the public beach down below and in front, beyond the marsh, all those cars and minivans parked just in the line of a perfect sight out to sea.

My mother would have loved this house. I always think of her when I am in the middle of a postcard, doing nothing but oohing and ahhing, which is what she liked best, the oohing and ahhing opening up a space in her you knew nothing could fill, that cannot be filled except with more longing—a summer view that can never actually be touched.

The first summer we spent at the Cape, Josh was still limping from his foot, which got damaged when he was in the hospital with croup. A night nurse stuck an IV into the tissue instead of a vein. We worried that the limp would be permanent. Zach was crawling around in his little sailor hat, chasing seagulls. Jerry and I, married just three years, were already grandparents twice. We sent Kelly and Doron out to eat and took care of both kids for the first time, a little scared, playing house as if we hadn't both had kids ourselves. I wanted to be the grandmother my mother didn't know how to be. Josh wanted to go out and look for roly-poly bugs, and we found ten of them under the rocks behind the cottage. We tried to give them names, but kept getting them mixed up. "Let's let them go home, now," Josh said, anxious for them when we were done.

Actually, this is about my mother, who has mostly managed to stay out of sight until now. You could have her in a room with all these people and she would be sitting on the couch, not able to think what to say, chewing her cuticle and jiggling her leg nervously. Or she would be sitting on the dock watching the minnows gather around her toes while the rest of us were swimming. Right now she is moving around awkwardly in the invisible past in the Central Lake cottage among the athletic, intellectual Browns. She and my father had only been married a few months when he was shipped out overseas and she went to the lake with his family. She was alone with them—daughter of a Shriner, church elder, and president of the Boone County Abstract Company, and his wife, member of the Garden Club and the ladies' Sunshine club. She told me once that "Daddy Brown," as no one but her ever called him, had dedicated himself that summer to trying to help her swim better. He would row the boat across the lake, with her floundering along beside him in the water. They all attempted in vain to teach her how to steer a canoe. When she hiked, she

93

stumbled over roots, preferred to sit on a blanket in the sun, drying her hair. She seemed always to need guidance, but was secretly anguished when Grandmother showed her how to do things. One of her favorite lines was, "If your grandmother hadn't died when she did, I wouldn't have been able to stay married to your father." All the time, she said she didn't know why she stayed married to him. But anyone could see why. She loved him as much as she hated him. And she was weak. Her frightened heart was invisible to my father. I can say this now.

For whatever reason, she endured sleeping summer after summer in the cottage bedroom separated by only a curtain from the living room. Sleeping in there with my father, with my retarded brother beside them in his crib and my sister and I whining and fighting right outside on cots in the living room. Listening to the boys upstairs, and to Aunt Cleone rattling around half the night next to them in the only bedroom with a door. And her in-laws across the way in the little green cottage, inventing rules everyone had to live by.

Unlike Kelly and Doron, the only vacation house I ever had as a child was this one, which has never changed. It still has the inscrutable picture of Henry George over the mantle. It has Miles Standish and Priscilla Alden behind the glass of the medicine cabinet in the living room. It has an old pump organ with a broken bellows. You have to pump like crazy, with one foot only, to get enough air to make a sound. The organ is in the living room, a few feet from the burlap curtains of the "bedroom." My sister and I are playing "Heart and Soul." No, we are seven and ten years old when we do this. We are bored. We decide to go back outside. We glance in through the curtains on our way out. It is midafternoon and our mother is lying on the bed, trying to escape. We do not pause. We head up the hill where we are building a little house under the trees. It is under a red berry bush. We have been told the berries are poison, which is very exciting. We have a row of twigs for a wall. We have a piece of bark on three rocks for a table. We stick two twigs through a leaf and make it stand up, for a headboard. We have a layer of leaves for the covers. We have mottled light for a ceiling. We can crawl part way under the bush, lie on our stomachs, and be the giant minds behind the workings of the universe. We put a poisonous berry on the table, dare each other to eat it. We are feeling edgy, risky, driven by an unspoken fury we are only the messengers for.

I have not described my mother. She doesn't want me to look closely at her because she used to be beautiful: long dark hair and dark eyes, perfect, pale skin, and a bosomy, shapely body. I have two photos of her that I try to keep in mind. One was taken soon after she was married. My father, I imagine, has put the pansy in her blown, slightly curly hair. Certainly, her face is upturned and she is smiling a sweet, hopeful smile at someone who has probably just told her she is beautiful. In the other photo, she is about thirty-five, regal, her hair up in a chignon. In black and white, her lips are blood red. There is, though, an upturning of the lips that I recognize, a dawning, a futility. I can hear her say to my father, the photographer, "Are you through yet?" a plea reverberating outward, far beyond this scene. Like Dorian Gray, she gradually crumpled into the outward reflection of her self-loathing. Her hearing shut down almost completely, her eyes jumped and floated, her senses all trying to escape.

She would rather I tell about her childhood. She was born in Maryville, Missouri. Her first years of school, she was sent away to Roachport, to live with an aunt, I think, because her parents thought the Maryville schools inferior. I may have the towns wrong, and I can't ask her now. I imagine she was terribly lonely. She said so once, but in a small voice, as if it no longer mattered. When her parents left the farm and moved to Columbia, the young Miss Simpich attended the College Training School, a rarified environment. She idolized her brother and her father. Her mother made her nervous, as she did me, always picking on some "unkemptness"—my nails, my hair—as if they symbolized a tragic flaw in an otherwise heroic being. I think my mother was raised to be a club woman, pretty and sweet, without opinions—the lady her father, the son of an immigrant cobbler, felt she should be. She and my father were next-door neighbors in Columbia, or they would never have met. My father hints that he wasn't sure he wanted to marry her. He said once that he had only suggested before he left for basic training that they might get married, and the next thing he knew, she sent him the engagement notice from the *Columbia Tribune*. Who knows if this is true? My father is not inclined to remember.

We are waiting for the last person to enter the dining room so they can all sit down. I am remembering only from waist-high, between the Browns and the Simpiches. Grandfather Brown is a ship's mast at a slight list, because of his lame leg. His thoughts unfurl for miles, taut above the turbulence of the conversation. Grandmother Brown is talking to Nana Simpich about pie, or soap, somewhere they can blessedly meet. Granddaddy Simpich's bald brow wrinkles with the strain of thinking what to say to the doctor, the dean, the former consultant to Roosevelt's brain trust. Like Silas Lapham in Howells's novel, Granddaddy's hands as they motion us to our seats move awkwardly as trussed hams. Look at this: they have all taken over. My mother chews her lip, caught inside their history.

The Simpiches' idea of a vacation was to take the Golden Eagle to Colorado Springs to see my uncle Bob. On their golden wedding anniversary, they went to Hawaii. They liked white tablecloths, sleeper berths, and leis. Nana frowned when we came back from Central Lake with a tan. "Little Indians," she called us. We learned from our father to be scornful of the Golden Eagle vacation. But at Central Lake, vacation was mostly for kids and men. They sailed and rowed while the women washed clothes in a tub. The men helped, but like children, not taking primary responsibility. I see my mother on the screened-in porch with Grandmother, Aunt Cleone, and maybe Aunt Lee, washing diapers. My father is carrying the soapy water up the hill to dump it so that it will filter through the soil before it reaches the lake. I hear her giggling just now, because she has splashed water all over her shirt. Oh, just when I have the scene built up to go a particular way, she is having a good time.

Years later, when Aunt Cleone got so that she didn't even realize when she was cold, my father wanted to let her sleep in the little cottage—which my parents had taken over by this time—where there was heat, but my mother refused. At last one of the invincible Browns was cracking. Although my mother took care of her when my father went off sailing, there was an edge in her kindness, an anger that came out in her pleasure at Cleone's confusion: "She spent half the day sorting silverware! She won't let me have her dirty clothes. She sleeps on top of her bed, she doesn't even know to crawl under the covers."

I am sure my mother would like to have Cleone out of this essay. My father's only sister was too much a presence in her life. For a year, when Cleone's husband Bob was out of a job, she and her three boys lived with us—all of us nonpaying

renters—in the Browns' house in Columbia while Grandfather was a guest lecturer for a year at another university.
Cleone was dedicated to convincing the world, including
my mother, to eat only natural foods, offering her own big,
healthy wrestling boys as evidence. I was only eight. Every
Monday I had don't-want-to-go-to-school stomach aches.
Aunt Cleone would stand at my bedroom door, taking over,
looking me over. She and I knew the truth. Where was my
mother, who was too timid to doubt me? I can't see her, except as they sit at the table tensely calculating how much
food each family ate, who should pay what portion of the
grocery bill. My father is out flying kites with the boys.

I am trying to see my mother now, but she is staring out the
window at nothing. I am trying to listen to her, but when
she speaks, it is in commonplaces: "You know you should
eat your green beans," or "Little girls shouldn't pick at their
noses," or "You have to wait two hours before you go in
swimming." When I ask why, she says, "Because you're supposed to." Her voice is a little girl's, repeating her parents'
admonitions. She had no quaint sayings. Being from Missouri, there were few pungent regionalisms in her speech.
"I'm just pooped," which she said all the time, comes about
as close as any I can think of. I think she thought in clichés.
I would like to believe, though, that in the dark crevices between the boulders of conventional phrases ran the current
of her very particular self—unarticulated, unthought, even.
This is the mother I did not know, could not know.

She is not in this summer house. She would have loved it. She would have loved to see her great-grandchildren grow so handsome. Everything would have been a picture book to her. She always wanted to go back to Cambridge, where they lived while my father was at Harvard. She would see pictures and long to be there again, although my father never took her anywhere. It must have been a good time for them, a young married couple. I have black-and-white photos of them clowning in the snow beside the Charles River, and one story, about a woman in their building who invited them up to dinner. They forgot and ate at home, and then remembered and went upstairs and ate again. This felt a little scary to me, the social obligation. The outside world was scary, as I sensed it, coming from my mother. She sent that woman a box of candy every Christmas until one year it was returned, no such person at that address.

When I was five, they spent a year in Middlebury, Vermont, where my father was teaching—a one-year job with potential for a tenure-track appointment that his father had arranged for him. According to the administration, their plans to hire on a tenure-track line changed, and my father's contract was not renewed. "They were so snooty," my mother said, "and I was just a girl from Missouri." Now I am the tenured professor, viewing my parents through those eyes. I see the frightened, immature young woman with no sense of where she was, what traditions, what obligations, would need to accompany her husband's appointment. I see my father, oblivious as well, angry, trapped in his father's life.

I see my mother with a cigarette in her mouth, trying that adult pleasure for the first time, modeling herself after a new friend down the street. My father is sarcastic, outraged. She throws out the cigarettes.

I have a letter from her to my aunt Cleone, who was unable to attend Grandmother Brown's funeral. It is an adult letter. It makes me ashamed of thinking of her as a child. She describes the polka-dotted dress they put on her for the funeral, and to be cremated in. She describes Beethoven on the phonograph, the roses, and the people who came. "Many people said she looked very nice. I think you would have been pleased," she wrote. I try to find more of her in the letter, but even in her rounded school-girl script, she is cautious, public.

The most public time of her life was after my brother Mark was in the nursing home and at last she was free to get a job. She went to work at the hospital nursery as a nurse's aide. For those few years, she was an expert on babies. She would demonstrate with her fingers how small the preemie was; she would describe the mothers anxiously attempting breast-feeding. She and the other aides would have lunch together, and gradually her speech became artificially punctuated with their intonations, their cuss words and crude jokes. Whatever it cost, she belonged to a community.

This is about the spaces that do not contain my mother. The summer places that do not admit you into their winter darkness, that have been waiting to show you only the face you came to see. If the house belongs to you, it has taken itself back over the winter. You approach it humbled, willing to work. If it is not your house, you are desperate to learn from its objects. You examine the lamps, doilies, and pieces of driftwood. Your fondest hope is that the paintings are real—no matter how horrible—not manufactured. You are looking for signs of life. The houses lack important elements, and you are proud of yourself when you learn to get along without them. This one has no bottle opener, but the end of the corkscrew substitutes. The lamp in our bedroom has the switch shaft missing; the screen is out in one window. And the terrible upstairs shower! Even though it is your vacation, you fix these things in your mind. You try not to, but you paint the house, buy matched dishes, and get two wicker chairs. If you stay for weeks, you begin redecorating your own house, the one you left behind, and building a rock walkway across the front, painting the window frames.

After my grandparents died, my parents started staying all summer at the lake, taking over the more convenient little green cottage. At nine or ten in the morning, my mother would still be in her quilted robe, eating toast and watching *The Today Show* or whatever came next, exactly as if she were at home. I would come in and sit down and she would turn the TV down reluctantly, cutting her eyes at it, more interested in Regis and Kathy Lee than in the real conversation, if you could call it that. My father would hold forth on the increasing property taxes, or propellers, or boat self-steering mechanisms. I would try to be interested, but my mother would quickly slip back to the comforting nest of TV sound. Sometimes when my father was out sailing, I would come sit with her on the deck. I would try to recall something in our past. "That was when Mark was getting worse and Daddy had lost his job and was spending the year alone in Missouri starting his new one. I was seventeen and crying every day about having to move and was out every night with Harry, and you were alone with all that. No wonder you needed gold salts injections for your arthritis," I said. "You must have been miserable." "Oh," she replied, "I don't know. I didn't think about it."

In spite of my lifetime of birthdays at the lake, I would have to get someone to remind her every year. Gifts were hard for my mother. Everyone else had everything and she had nothing—I think she felt that—so giving seemed futile to her, and receiving only reminded her of her lack. Her brother Bob made character dolls and Christmas ornaments. He designed an angel to look like Mother, and she sobbed helplessly when she opened it, face-to-face briefly with undeniable testimony of her presence in the world. Her last summer at the lake, she gave each of her daughters identical gifts—as usual—this time one of Bob's porcelain doll–face ornaments, something I would never buy. "She thinks you don't like it," my sister told me, so I pulled it out and showed it off in front of her to anyone who stopped in. But I imagine she knew. What can I say in my defense? I wanted a gift that was about me, not her. I, who had so much already, wanted her to acknowledge my own existence.

I thought her selfish, too, for refusing to stop on the way home that year to see Aunt Cleone in the nursing home. Soon Cleone's mind would be entirely out of reach, but for now, she would have appreciated a visit from her brother, and possibly from Mother. But all Mother could think about was getting home. Looking back, I am sure that she'd begun to have small, almost imperceptible strokes. She felt her own mind beginning to collapse internally and wanted to be on home territory when it happened.

I think she was briefly aware of me when I got to the Cape Girardeau hospital just before she slipped into her final coma. At least she was aware of the gravity of the occasion. Her eyes teared up, all three of her daughters bending over her, saying, "Mother, we're here." After she was deep in a coma, they ran her through the MRI to prove there was no brain activity left. I have imagined her a hundred times, claustrophobic, helplessly encased in the tube she was so afraid of. What if she was more aware than we imagined, and terrified? The last few days, the nurse would come in and say very loudly into her ear, "Mrs. Brown, I am going to suck out the liquid in your lungs now," explaining to us that the hearing is the last to go. So we took turns going up to her and saying "I love you" into her ears, loudly, awkwardly.

The call came about 4 a.m. that she was "having trouble breathing," but my father didn't wake us up and didn't go himself. Maybe he was afraid, or thought that in her condition, it wasn't important to rush over. Her aloneness in that bare, temporary room, with nothing that belonged to her, pulls at me, something unfinished. Actually, I have to say, it infuriates me. My powerlessness infuriates me. Just as I do with the MRI, I imagine her waking up, as people supposedly sometimes do, before her death, for one shining moment aware, fully present—and alone. The lighted room, intended to signify attention in the midst of darkness, is a limbo of hums and clicks. The space of the hospital room— that small, white enclosure—comes to me and asks me to wait. To be patient. She will say something; I will reply.

"Oh, it is too late, too late!" she had cried to me over the phone two years earlier. "Your father has taken all the money he got from that state retirement settlement and put it in a CD, and it's my fault. I let him do it. Now I'll never get to go to the Grand Canyon. At first he said he'd take me, but then I let him put the money in a CD, and he won't ever take it out." "Look, just call the travel agent and book the hotel," I said. "He'll go." But she was afraid. The one time I got there myself, it was fogged over. The great yawning Canyon is still waiting for both of us to see it.

None of the rest of us liked open caskets, but she had always said she did. It was what you were supposed to have. So. In it was some adult woman with a strangely straight mouth, a quiet, determined jaw, a person who might have been my mother, under other circumstances.

Kelly and Doron leave for the restaurant, and the house takes on the quality of waiting that is always present when parents are gone, exaggerated by being away from home, in a "beach house." The kids are glad to be with us, but they keep an ear tuned for the car grinding up the shell driveway, for the door opening. Jerry and I put Noah down for bed at 7:30, then Jerry reads to Josh on his bed and I read to Zach on his, our voices overlapping. Josh wants a soccer story, being somewhat of a star himself, his foot fully healed, but with a huge, spread-eagle scar. Zach wants a book that has short rhymes at the bottom of each page, telling what objects you are supposed to find in the clouds, or the forest, or the city scene. He is quicker at this than I am. A cloud looks like a cloud until Zach shows me how to make it into a three-masted schooner, sailing among other surprising objects. Afterward, Jerry and I go downstairs and straighten up. We make the place ours, as if we were at home and these were our own children upstairs. As if we had been married to each other, not to other people, when our own children were this young. As if things had been this happy from the start. My mother has disappeared from the story again. She likes watching from the sidelines. She is sitting on the dock swirling her feet in the water. "Look," I point out to her, "there's a three-masted schooner in that cloud. Zach found it." "Oh yes," she says, "There it is!" We are oohing and ahhing over that versatile cloud.

Relativity for Dummies

Barefoot, still in his pajamas, he wanders out of the rain into the big cottage, holding his book spread-winged like holy scripture, or a dead bird: "Okay, look, Maxwell's predictions are supposed to be the same for all observers. Take electromagnetic waves—including light—that travel at, say, speed c. All observers are supposed to measure the same value of c for the speed of light—even if they're moving with respect to each other!"

His tall body blocks the light. He's rigid as a heron, but with the slight lean of an old spine beginning to curve in on itself. In full swing now, Professor Brown captures a class once again. He hitches up his pajama bottoms absentmindedly.

"Carried to its silliest extreme, you have one twin leaving Earth on a spaceship. Supposedly, less time elapses for him, and he returns younger than the one who remained! Good grief." He runs his hand through his gray-white hair and grins like a schoolboy. He's been studying this issue for years—still not convinced.

It's 8:30 in the morning. We've just come in from our swim, dripping wet—all three of his daughters. He's turned mostly toward me. Being the oldest and the most academic, I tend to get pelted with Einstein the most. About all I can say is "Daddy, I think you're really smart, but I don't know, you could be wrong. If it turns out twenty years from now you're proven right, I'll erect a gold Academy Award statue on top of your tombstone, I promise." I have to think about the number of years, because I'm on the downside of fifty myself. I'm dying to get my hair dry. Only one of us can turn on the dryer at a time, because the wiring is older than I am.

The week or so we're here in Michigan, the three of us turn into teenagers, rolling our eyes at our father, giggling and daring each other to get in the cold water. We're terribly much alike—all English teachers of various kinds, all slim, originally dark-haired, though we have to do things to it now to keep it dark, and older than we look. We each have two children—Millie's and mine grown now—and we're each married to successful and orderly men, the opposite of our father. We each work very hard. And we're very different.

Millie's always been witty. To make matters worse, she used to look like Jane Fonda: huge brown eyes, milky skin, straight dark hair. When she was a student, she won "Best Dressed Woman on Campus." She was so perfect that she stayed a virgin until she married and is still happily married to the same man thirty years later. Michelle, born fourteen years after me, was the wild one, bleached hair and blood-red fingernails, until she married. She used to think she wanted to be a model and actually did go to Barbizon for a year—she's stately, pale-skinned, slim as a ballerina. I was the one with pimples and thick glasses. I've had my troubles, but I'm okay after a lot of therapy and meditation.

When I'm not meditating, I'm trying to figure things out. I brought a book to the lake this year, *Why Christianity Must Change or Die*, by an Episcopal bishop. I forgot to mention I'm also an Episcopalian, more or less, when I can ignore most of the dogma. In this book, Bishop Spong explains that we need to demythologize Christianity, divest it of its trappings, even divest our religion of its superhuman deity, to find the Ground of Being once again. So to find God, we have to get rid of God. I like that. My sisters like that. My father, being an atheist, likes that. We all read the book, although my father wanders in, wanting to know if I can make any sense of "Ground of Being." I tell him it's intuitive. He goes away and looks up intuitive, trying to make sure of what I mean. He comes back. I'm washing dishes.

"It means understood without the use of reason," he says, scratching his head and looking like he ate the canary. "A contradiction in terms, if you ask me." He dries the electric skillet, his hands a tangled rope of veins.

This is the kind of battle we have, now—quiet, almost tender, stepping carefully around buried explosives.

His aging, which he finds a great nuisance, is increasingly an explosive. As is its objective correlative, the cottage, bought the year he was born. The three of us daughters have to figure out soon what to do with it—sell it or keep it. It needs everything—a roof and a paint job, first. Last night a slow drip hit the other side of my bed. I was too sleepy to bother with it, so I just stayed on my own side. And there's no plumbing, no running water.

On this particular morning, we went swimming in the rain, since there was no lightning. It's really wonderful to be up to your neck in cold water, watching more water pock-mark the surface, feeling invincible because you can't get any wetter or colder. And then to come in to the fireplace, Michelle's kids, nine and eleven, sitting in front of it, wait-ing for us to feed them again even though they've already had Frosted Flakes. It makes you feel heroic, deserving of the fire, deserving of the entire evolutionary process that provides matches, electric stoves, hot oatmeal. It makes me feel merged with my grandmother whose ashes were thrown in the lake I swim in, who could swim all the way to Snowflake, a resort across the lake, until the day she died.

So I had mentioned on this particular morning while we were swimming.

"Snowflake was Spiritualist camp, wasn't it?" Millie had asked. "What's a Spiritualist?" I was supposed to know, be-ing the spiritual one.

Your head's above water when you do the breast stroke, so you can talk and swim at the same time. "Well, there was Madame Blavatsky, who made roses appear in the air and walked through walls," I'd said, avoiding the question I didn't know the answer to. "The nineteenth century got to feel so sterile, so hopeless, with Darwin and all. There were these pockets of relief, I guess."

We'd all looked down the lake toward Snowflake, its beach now dotted with beached jet skis and inner tubes. A vision had come to me then of a fire on the sand at night, a small group of lit faces chanting, hands raised into the infinite. I like anything, true or not, that says a pox on all your logic.

We each in succession dry our hair. Sarah, Michelle's child, comes back from the outhouse whining, "It's wet in there!" Michelle goes up to check, and sure enough, the roof is leaking a steady stream over the hole that has a real toilet seat fastened to it, and a smaller trickle over the old wooden hole that I personally favor. There's nothing to do about it now. All a person can do is take an umbrella and a towel, wipe the seat off, and sit there trying to hold the umbrella open enough in the small space to keep the rain off.

This points up the seriousness of our problem. Forget trying to persuade our father to spend money on the place, although he has enough. And it belongs also to his brother, who doesn't want it, and his sister, who's in a nursing home. After they're gone, it goes to all eight grandchildren. Impossible to make a move without everyone's approval. None of the three of us sisters can afford to buy it outright from the others. And the taxes get worse every year. It's like a faceless corporation, corrupting before our eyes with no one to look to, no one to blame.

While I'm working on the breakfast dishes, Daddy comes in again, still reading aloud. This seems to be his morning for it. It doesn't help matters that as I try to open the lever on the hose to run water into the plastic dishpan, it spews all over the counter and floor. This is because we have fifty feet of hose that runs from the outside spigot of the little cottage, where Daddy and his lady friend Rebecca stay, through the kitchen window of the big cottage. Needless to say, the little cottage has running water, installed years ago for our aging grandparents. When the lever's been closed for a while, the hose builds up pressure and spews all over the place. I shouldn't have to live like this, even for a week, I think. Furthermore, I have no patience with the theory of relativity, but I'm an invisible sounding board, doomed to listen, required to respond.

"Okay, imagine I'm standing by the roadside equipped with a device for measuring the speed of light. The device uses a very fast clock to time the passage of light over a distance of exactly one meter. Are you with me so far?" he asks.

I try to hold this in my mind. I'm standing there by the roadside with something that looks like a stopwatch. I can see myself, but the language drifts away after that. I feel the way I did in the sixth grade reading story problems, blankly terrified.

"Okay," I say. "Go on."

"You drive by in a car at seventy miles per hour equipped with an identical apparatus. Down the road, a traffic signal flashes, and we both measure the speed of light as it passes us. Despite the fact that we're in relative motion, we both get exactly the same speed for the light," he reads.

The drainer's getting piled too high to continue to wash, and I'm not getting any help here.

"We get the same results if we repeat the experiment with you going past in a jet plane at 600 miles per hour or even in a space craft at half the speed of light." He's beginning to get that triumphant gleam. I know my role.

"How can this be?" I reply, dutifully.

"It means," he says, sneering, "that supposedly our measures of time and space have to be different. Time and space are not absolute, but are relative to the particular observer."

As usual, I'm desperately thinking what to say. "That doesn't make any sense to me," is the right answer, because he agrees wholeheartedly.

Millie comes in and starts drying dishes, saving me. Daddy wanders out, hair flopping as he leans over the book. Generally he slicks his hair back with some kind of hair goop, but in the summer he sometimes doesn't bother. We all think he looks better with his hair soft and waving; however, arranging hair is low on his agenda. Truth is high. He's still arguing with my uncle Bob, my mother's brother, about religion. Bob has been trying to convert him for forty years, and Daddy continues to write him long letters in refutation. Bob actually believes in Creationism, which makes Daddy choke with horror, but it keeps him interested in life.

By the time we've finished the dishes, the sun's come out. The three of us take our cups of tea and sit in the one patch of sunlight left since all the trees have been allowed to grow up unpruned. We're trying to warm up from our swim. Michelle wants to buy the cottage, but she lives in Texas, her husband isn't interested in coming, and she can't afford to pay for the place alone. She doesn't say much, so full of longing she is. When she was a child, our parents had the longest spell ever of not coming to the lake because Daddy built a sailboat too large to bring to Michigan. For most of her childhood, they camped out at Kentucky Lake so that he could sail that boat. She feels she missed out on her spiritual inheritance, and now it may be sold out from under her.

Millie shifts nervously, sipping her tea. She and her husband have bought a thirty-foot sailboat, moored on Grand Traverse Bay. Too big for this little lake. They love to travel and don't want the hassle of this poor old cottage. I get the feeling she'd like to leave all this behind her.

I don't know about me. This place is beyond love or hate for me, beyond any clear vision. I don't know whether it's the part of me better left behind in childhood—or whether it's like one of my arms or legs, moving with me into adulthood, not the same cells, but still my own dear arm or leg. I'm thinking of Howards End, the way Forster has Mrs. Wilcox and then Meg, the only real characters in the book, draw their meaning from hanging onto the old house itself. I know that the three of us sisters see different cottages in our minds. Cottage As Abstraction—which is why it's falling apart.

"He came in just as I was getting the new curtains up in the kitchen," Michelle begins. "He started in—'Oh my God. You girls expect me to spend $15,000 to fix this place up.' Sure. The estimate we got for painting was $800! I just spent $20 for curtains. Suddenly it's $15,000 to fix the cottage. Who's rational?"

"He'd rather imagine the worst, so he can get his way." I say this, knowing that in a way, I'm the angriest. I'm the oldest. There was no older sibling to blunt the effect of our parents on me. They were both children, and I was the worried parent, trying to mitigate the damage of their fits and fights. I have a reason to be angry. But it's a peaceful kind of anger now, cooked down with all the other feelings in a kind of vegetable soup.

Millie closes her eyes to the sun, lies back on the pine needles and soft grass. She'd just as soon not deal with this. Sarah and Daniel come out and wallow around on us as if we were interesting playground equipment, laps for nesting and shoulders for climbing on. They're bored, and Sarah, being the oldest, is interested in watching the complexities of these relationships, so vital to her mother. She brushes her golden hair in the sunlight.

"I think we should paint the cottage yellow," she says, not letting things die. "With green trim."

Michelle agrees. "A butter yellow."

Now I am not in favor of this because it would probably mean an extra coat, to cover the white adequately. And it would mean repainting the porches, too. There's nothing wrong with the white. I foresee an avalanche of decisions, everyone's taste and agenda conflicting, stretching us to the edges of our love for each other. I feel tired. Michelle is younger, still inclined to change the world.

I understand a little. When I first started coming to the cottage again after almost twenty years away, I wanted desperately to buy it, to fix it up, to keep it for myself forever. The cottage was me, the me who got lost during two terrible marriages.

It is a slow morning. Days here often move from breakfast to lunch without any intermediate activity. Just swim, dress, cook, eat, wash dishes, drink tea and talk and talk, then make lunch. Time at the lake is different. For one thing, days are longer in the north. We stay up later and later, sleep later in the morning. Eventually, we're getting up at nine, having breakfast at 10:30, lunch at three and dinner at nine. It feels perfectly normal, each activity relative only to the next, not to an outside authority. The time between 1918, when our grandparents bought the cottage, and now is subsumed in the slapping of waves against rocks, the same rocks in a literal sense, the same waves in the sense that the basin of the lake continues to hold the moisture that pours in from a thousand small streams, the result of an endless birth and rebirth of evaporation and condensation.

We're still sitting in the patch of sunlight when Daddy wanders over, raving in his newer, milder, older way. The kids have been fishing off his sailboat and have left dirt from the worms all over, including on his new Dacron sails. As usual he feels helpless. So he's bundled up the sails and is carrying them inside, a petulant child taking his toys home. "You can't wash sails, you know," he says as if we were all idiots, "because of the sliders." He's chewing his tongue in the old familiar way. Michelle makes the kids go clean out the boat, feeling, I know, like a child herself—irresponsible, abandoning generations of superior child-rearing.

"We could rent out the little cottage after Daddy dies," Michelle says. "That would at least pay the taxes."

"You're three thousand miles away. Who's going to take care of the place?" I ask, hating to dash her hopes. The problems are endless, as I see them. Still, the map I have in my head of my world has two pins stuck in it, one in Delaware and one in Michigan. I can't imagine the Michigan pin removed. I used to have nightmares of the lake dried up. I don't say any of this, for fear of encouraging Michelle.

At last the sun reaches the end of the dock, and it seems better to sit out there in the broad air. Ducks gather around us, six of them at first, then four more—a mother and three babies—waiting for the bread steadily forthcoming from the kids. We watch the ducks turn up their tails, beaks down, giving up and eating some grasses, I guess, off the bottom. The kids get them tame enough to almost eat out of their hands, then fall comes and hunting season. They don't have a chance. But every year ducks show up. Who knows how many are the same ones, how many die?

The wind's come up enough, so Daddy's put the sails back on. He and Rebecca are going sailing. In the last years, Mother didn't want to go, and was so weak anyway she had to be hoisted on and off. He's got himself someone who'll go nearly every time now, even though she often forgets she's been, being in the early stages of senile dementia. Daddy drifts the boat right next to the dock to pick her up. She's a sweet lady, but too much like our mother for comfort: always trying hard, but held down by the shackles of insecurity and depression. She's even plump like our mother. But Daddy says she likes sex, which is a big plus for him. We tell him to shut up about this, but it does no good.

It's a relief to have Daddy occupied with a woman, though. We can let him have his life and not think about it too much. None of us has been to his house in Missouri since Mother died. Judging from the little cottage, we know what it looks like—a ghastly heap of papers, books, magazines, dishes, rags, and electric motor parts. Probably by now you'd have to dig a path through, the way they had to do in his sister's house before she went to the nursing home. If we sent in a cleaning crew, they wouldn't know where to start, and Daddy would chase them out with a broom, anyway, if he could find one.

The wind's up, from the north, which is good, but it's pretty strong. The boat looks great with its new sails, headed across the lake on its first tack, at a tilt, sun glinting off the waves. We can see both dark bodies, both heads of white hair.

So the afternoon starts out as not much, which suits us fine. We make a grocery list and drive in to Prevo's. We buy a large soup pot at the hardware store and make up a story to tell Daddy—that I brought it from home because we had two and didn't need it. It's awful, I know, for grown women to tell fibs like this to their father, but believe me, we know the consequences of truth. This is better. We stop at a gift and toy shop so the kids can spend the money that's burning a hole in their pockets. They buy junk—puppets that will have their strings broken or hopelessly tangled in a matter of hours. We come home and swim, although it's not as much fun after the waves are up. They slap you in the face.

We're just out when Michelle yells that she hears the phone ringing in the little cottage. I dash over, still in my swimsuit. It rings long enough for me to get there, so it has to be family—someone who knows how it is here with phones.

"Hello, this is the Sheriff's office. Is this one of Mr. Brown's daughters?"

"Yes," I say, quickly sinking into a mercifully numb zone.

"Your father and Mrs. Whiting have had a boating accident. They're fine. We'll be bringing them home in a few minutes. Someone has pulled the boat to shore and is looking after it. We'll let you know where it is later."

When things are out of your control, they seem to move more slowly, to circle through your consciousness almost lazily, while you watch. "Well, this is a new one," is all I'm conscious of. "A new development. Oh." It's probably adrenaline that does this, but I always thought adrenaline speeds things up. Maybe if you speed up a whole lot, the effect is of slowing down. Daddy would probably know.

All five of us form a receiving line in the clearing where the cars are parked when they drive up. Michelle's trembling. I worry about how often she does that. Millie's keeping one hand on each of the kids.

Daddy sheepishly helps Rebecca out of the patrol car. They're both wrapped in blankets, top half, both barefoot. Daddy still has the legs of an athlete, veins standing out against the muscle, but he balances on them carefully, I notice, almost as if he were on tiptoe.

"Here." He unwraps his blanket and hands it back. "Thank you very much. I'm warm enough now," he says as if he were delivering a lecture. The patrolman and I exchange a look that I know someday some two people will exchange about me—the look that says "We're in charge now. His day is over. Let us be gentle, but let us move in and take over." There's a moment that has been building all his life, all our lives, that comes at last: not a hormonal shift, the kind my sisters and I discuss endlessly; not a financial one, or even exactly one that's all about health. At a certain point, there's a look. No one—not my father, even—could fail to see it, I will not fail to see it when it comes for me. Gentle as it is, it contains a vein of naked aggression, a payback for all the suffering caused, for the loneliness of childhood, for the strain and self-sacrifice of adulthood. "It's your fault," the look says. "I love you. You've tried your best, I know you didn't mean to, but all the sins of Adam came to rest on you and then you gave birth to me, and here I am, struggling." And we're all the kinder for the flicker of that thought. Our voices take on a slightly careful tone, not quite patronizing. If we're sensitive, we take care not to patronize.

"What happened?" Millie asks as soon as the car's driven away.

"Oh it was so silly. It was my fault," he says, ducking his head like a child. "I tacked a little too much into the wind. I should've lowered the jib, or at least loosened it. The wind was stronger than I thought. The boat went over."

A mistake in sailing. This never would have happened ten years ago, I think quickly, with that floating, out-of-control feeling again.

"Rebecca, how did you—" I couldn't imagine her thrown into that cold water.

"Oh, I was fine," she says in that breezy way she has of moving past her moments of forgetfulness. "I just swam until they got me out."

I keep forgetting she has a degree in physical education. I get her too mixed up with Mother.

"I was worried about your father," she adds. "He was so cold."

"Someone called 911 and they actually sent an ambulance," he says. "So silly, but I guess that's what they do in such situations. So they put me in the back of the ambulance and took my vital signs. My teeth were chattering so much I couldn't answer their questions very well." He stretches to show how calm he is now and almost knocks a pot of impatiens off the deck railing.

"It's a good thing we tipped over near enough to town that people saw us," he goes on. "I don't know how long I could have lasted in that water." I'm surprised he says this. I don't think he says it for effect.

"Where's the boat?" I want to know, sure that it is his main concern.

"Well that's the amazing part," he says, his eyes growing rounder. "Some people came out in motorboats and dragged the boat to shore. I don't know how they ever got it upright with the heavy wooden mast, but they did. And they got a pump and pumped it out. Some people even went back and fished all the life jackets and cushions out of the lake and brought them back to the boat. As far as I can see, nothing was lost. People kept stopping by the ambulance to see if we were okay. They even wanted to feed us."

It makes me teary, but I get teary more easily the older I get. "Look," I want to point out to him, "you can relax a little. It's okay to get old. See, the world will hold you up." But I'm not the one who's just been humiliated.

I get teary whenever it dawns on me for a few minutes that I don't have to try so hard. That's what I want to say to him: relax. In those moments I feel as if no matter how fast the Earth's traveling, no matter how much time's shifting and moving on, I'm stretched out in a hammock—say, the old canvas one in front of the cottage—swung between the dualities: the multiple, material arms of the human race and the invisible Ground of Being. It's a comfort, like not being able to escape the speed of light. If Einstein said we can't, who am I to argue? It's a good resting place, anyway—the speed of light.

I heard Bishop Spong speak last spring, right after I'd read *Why Christianity Must Change or Die*. He said he was a good friend of the scientist Carl Sagan. Sagan, being a devout atheist, was always pointing out the absurdities of Christianity. Once at a party, Sagan chased Spong all the way across the room to tell him this one. "Okay," he said, "Jesus lifts off from the Earth at his ascension. Assume he's traveling 186,000 miles per second, the speed of light. At this moment, he still hasn't cleared the galaxy!"

I tell Daddy this one after dinner. Laughing makes him feel better, I think, along with the pie made from the tart cherries we'd picked two days ago at King's Orchard. The kids got carried away and picked more than we can possibly use before they spoil. This is the way nature is: it dumps more on you at once than you can use, then later you have to be content with memories. Like the sunset, flooding everything with pink light. We've taken hundreds of photos of it off the end of the dock, trying to keep it a little longer.

"Look at the sunset," we say, finishing our pie, not because anyone could possibly fail to look at it, but because the words add weight to the attention, give it gravity.

I tell Michelle that being at the cottage right now is an exercise in living in the moment—you can't take ownership, you just have to use it the way you use a life, live inside it until it's over. Sit here on the screened-in porch eating pie, be aware of sitting here, feel the strong gravitational pull and let it slow time down for you.

Supposedly.

Daddy typed out Einstein's version of this theory on a scrap of paper a couple of days ago. My job is to study it and report back:

> Light loses energy climbing away from a gravitational mass. It can't slow down, but the frequency of the light waves is reduced. To an observer looking toward a region of strong gravity, the effect is to see time running slower in that region. This is called gravitational time dilation.

I pull out the paper and read it again. I nearly have it memorized, and I still don't get it. If you're there, in that region, are you actually younger? Does time actually slow down? Einstein says it depends on where you're watching from. The trouble is, I'm here. I can only watch from here, ever.

To Tell a Story

EXULTATION is the going
Of an inland soul to sea,—
Past the houses, past the headlands,
Into deep eternity!

Bred as we are, among the mountains,
Can the sailor understand
The divine intoxication
Of the first league out from land?

—Emily Dickinson

It's pitch black now. I'm sitting with maybe sixty or seventy other kids on the huge flat rocks below the spillway. Bonfire's gone to embers, one of the counselors is playing a guitar, and we've reached the end of "Jacob's Ladder." They have us theatrically softening down the last phrase, "children of the cross," before we leave in silence for our cabins. Bo Parker's had his arm on my back throughout, more or less. He's angled it in such a way that it could be there to balance himself, but it is the bonfire of my passion, the crux of my cross, my Jacob's ladder, my Star in the East. I am suffused with religion.

In 1958, maybe still, the smartest thing a church could do with thirteen-year-olds was to herd them together, give them a clear regimen, and steer their sexual restlessness, at least temporarily, toward Jesus. I went to church camp the three summers of junior high. A group of us from our local church and others of our denomination in the state were driven over the Boston Mountains, down a rough gravel road, to the woods below Lake Fort Smith. It was a typical camp: little wooden cabins, central dining hall, stone paths between. What I loved most was the orderliness. If you felt socially awkward, there was safety in shifting to the next activity at the hollow clang of the cowbell. I especially loved the early morning prayer-walks when we were told to take our Bibles, pencils, and paper and meander silently by ourselves along the paths, to think, pray, read, and take notes. Sunrise, Jesus, and a notepad: the happy conjunction promoted by the First Christian Church (Disciples of Christ) in Fayetteville, Arkansas. You could write poems to God. Hellfire was someone else's idea, not ours. Burning of any sort, even fervent religious burning, was not the way we did things. Nonetheless, I burned. What I burned for was ambiguous. For love, for sex, for God. How to separate them? Each is a longing for a particular moment when the universe opens: for a merging. And that last sentence is embarrassingly nonsensical, if you lived in my family.

I am nine years old. Nana and Mother trap me between them on the edge of the bed. Nana is wearing her flowered housedress. Mother humps her shoulders, anxious to say the right thing in front of her own mother. This is her daily cross, since we're all living next door to each other for now while my father finishes graduate school. They ask me if I would like to "join the church" this Easter. That's the expression they use. They would never say, "Take Jesus as your savior." They would never unbolt the door behind which the hydra-headed beast of the emotions snuffled and pawed the ground. Better use code. I am cowed by what I perceive behind the door. I say okay. I am already a child with a vast binary life. In the wildly secret half, Jesus and God live in the Rockies. I, turbaned, drag across the Sahara, weeping for rain. Or sometimes I wear a nun's habit, stretch out every night on a bed of stone, kneel every morning on a stone floor with bloody knees. I make no sound from that romantic life, so as not to give myself away. "Yes," I say. Together, they smile as if I had just said "Thank you," unbidden, to a stranger. They ask my little sister. She is only six, but she says okay too, because I did. They make us taffeta dresses, with white ruffles.

Protestants are logocentric. Even in the throes of early Methodism they looked to the rational Word to explain and justify their faith. Logocentric thinking has three characteristics: First, you discriminate and justify things by a God (or something God-like) who stands outside the system ("In the beginning was the Word."); second, you follow logical principles to structure your experiences; and third, you hold to binary distinctions: form-matter, reason-emotion, God-Devil. Even Paul's conversion is described as binary: a before and an after. First a persecutor of Christians, then a convert; first blinded, then visionary, and so on. God, outside the system, justifies the system.

My church, in general, was as rational as the Presbyterians but without the severity, as doctrinairily easy-going as the Methodists but without an official creed. On Sunday mornings back when we lived in Missouri, Nana would put on a hat with a hint of a veil and clamp her fox's teeth to the tail curved around her neck. Granddaddy would be going over his elder's prayer, the most literary act of his adult life. He would ask Nana if she thought it was okay. Then we would go, my mother, Nana, Granddaddy, and my sister. We sat on the American flag side instead of the Christian flag side, aligned with the power of America. My father the atheist stayed home.

I always felt our church was a little embarrassed by its own mission. It preached love and kindness and the Jesus who had a perfectly respectable message. If we all paid attention to it, our lives would be better. The God of my church had some good ideas and gave them to Moses. God was male, but the kind of father who barely looks over the top of the newspaper to tell the kids it's okay if they go to the movies. He expects they'll be good kids. He raised them. The peaks and valleys of Heaven and Hell seemed like romance, relegated in sermons to dependent clauses. The only righteous indignation left to us was hearing the creed if we visited a neighboring church; "No creed but Christ" was our creed. What *about* Christ was left up to us, and as for me, I preferred God, who was clearly Invisible, Almighty, and Omniscient. Christ reminded me of my mother, long-suffering, unable to extricate herself from her unhappy life.

God, on the other hand, was the best kind of God, one who would stay just out of reach, leaving me panting with longing. Somewhat the way, probably, that I loved my own father, at home puttering around in his private world of peat pots, petunias, tomatoes, and broken clocks to fix, or reading Darwin and Einstein, laughing out loud at Twain's *Letters from the Earth*. My father was absolutely certain that natural science, the brainchild of logocentricism, demonstrated what it means to be human. Nurtured on the nineteenth-century doctrine of positivism, his father had taught him that the paradigm for gaining proper knowledge is science. Yet my father, unable to assert himself in the midst of Christians, decided that his daughters would be better off going to church with their mother, because then, at least, unlike him, they'd fit in.

I was "split at the root," as the poet Adrienne Rich says of her own life. Evidence my own baptism. On the Saturday before, we go to the church to rehearse with the other kids. First there would be the part on Sunday morning when we had to say I *do*, that we did take Jesus. I was relieved that my part consisted of only two words. Then in the afternoon would be my baptism, by immersion. This is how it goes: I walk down the four heavy steps, soaking the ruffles my grandmother sewed on my dress. Someone has tied the maroon curtains aside; the little concrete pool waits at the end of the stretch of stairs, staged white and public with light, empty cross rising above it like a mast. It's waited for me behind velvet the way Jesus has waited, patiently, tenderly, the way Dr. Lemon waits, robe billowing in water, words tensed for lift-off. He locks the mask of his handkerchief over my nose, and I am tipping backward toward the Three Names, unalterable, adult as pillars.

Though as soon as I get the water between heaven and me, my mind cuts loose. It's swimming under there like an old carp scathed from battle, skin hanging like ruffles. A carp, this is what I'll be, dark and nameless. Whatever I make up exists. More electric than Sunday or Easter, my secret life stays under, the swoosh, like the *cockadoodledo* the ear, nose, and throat doctor has me say as he syringes out the mucus from my nose, the sound that loosens things up. All I have to do is make that noise and keep it going. I keep on, out of range. Lovely, the drift of my hand, my imperial body, mine to drown or not, my secret heart and lungs, my collection of organs speaking to each other in the quiet ceremony of their own language, never needing to come up for air. You have to be a mystic or a poet to be seduced by any of this.

And so my sister and I became members of the church, which meant about the same to us as if we had indeed said "thank you" when asked to say it.

Notice in the preceding two paragraphs the burst of poetic language, then my quick turn out of it. Certain chemicals must have been released in my brain by the pictorial memory of baptism, stimulating my right brain, temporarily dislodging logical sequencing. One result of logocentrism has been to think we can explain all mental activities by finding their referents at the level of brain activity. However, our consciousness of having done so is another thing altogether. We're confounded by consciousness, which spoils the sea of tranquility we call "objectivity." We can't make sense of how consciousness evolved, how it's maintained by certain types of brain processing but not by others. Maybe it's just a product of some clever manipulation of images in the brain. Or maybe it's an illusion foisted on us by Descartes: that the intellect alone can perceive what is or what isn't. Or maybe Logos has trapped us into its safely linked-together boxcars traveling the rails of time, while consciousness is attending a pulpit-thumping revival service.

My friend Sharon Lyddon's family took me to revival services at the Church of Christ in their old boat of a car. I was their project. People with my sensible religion were always projects for those who soared and plunged to renew themselves. We looked as if we needed it, I guess. In the early morning mist, five days in a row in the summer, I went to her white clapboard church. Of course I got religion. They have you facing front, they pour it in you, and you have no say in the matter. There were the little tracts I brought home and read every word of. I read the Bible verses for the next day. I studied as if I were taking a class and I passed with flying colors, half convinced at last that maybe it would be better to have plain voices singing instead of instruments that get between you and God. "My Jesus, I Love Thee, I Know Thou Art Mine," bounced against the walls. I was certain the angels sang a capella.

My own church was arched with dark oak: oak and order, dignity and quiet, the kind of place to secretly fall in love in. I fell in love with every minister. Then there was Bo Parker from Paris, Arkansas. On the spillway rocks at church camp, I turned to him, desperate for a kiss, and scared him off. He decided to fall in love with one of the counselors. Wounded beyond words, I lay still as a saint's statue on my bunk, to steady the churning inside me. I constructed prayers with an instinctive faith that if I could line up words, one by one, they would fill the void. I read the Bible; its rhythm and its vocabulary, they comforted me.

A comforting verbal wrap-up to that little incident—but the closer I attend to my own story, the more I deconstruct it. That is, I can't help bringing contradictions and paradoxes to light. Bo Parker thought of me after church camp, wrote me a letter full of gentleness and apology. And my father, besides being a rationalist, is also a romantic, a dreamer, a poet. My weak mother was also a fighter for happiness, stronger than she knew. The afternoon of my baptism, I did also feel close to Jesus, flushed with light. I've found a way to make sense of things by selecting certain facts (out of the multitude) to make up a tale—a story of the Progress of My Spirit. Pure science can't choose this way. It knows that choosing itself distorts the truth. Heisenberg demonstrated that even the act of attention upon an object or event changes it. Yet wistfully, I hope to hold "true" in some sense, to make meaning public, not private.

Public and private have to bump into each other, to provide the context for meaning. When I was seventeen I went to the fortune-teller at the county fair. She held my palm and told me generalities that were pretty certain to hold true. I had on a wedding ring and didn't look as if I had children, so she told me I was having trouble getting pregnant because I had a "crooked uterus." She was right, maybe. She told me I would travel to the sea. She was right, eventually. Being at that age already in love with metaphor, I made her words correspond perfectly. The rest of the day, I remained a little giddy from my brief encounter with the mysterious and public universe's private message for me.

I longed for, I'd have given anything for, the two worlds to match. I have not been entirely forthcoming about my father. He hated religion, but he let himself be baptized, for my mother's sake. In the course of things, he went to church with her, and when they asked him to be a deacon, he didn't know how to say no. Sundays, he would drive to church, jaw muscles tightening. His anger scared me. "Someday I'm going to throw the communion tray to the floor and leave," he said. I checked the barometer of his anger every Sunday, watching for the triggering event that would finally do us in, uncover the chasm between our public and private lives. I measured by the intensity of his jaws. One Sunday he reported that his academic dean, who was also an elder in our church, had asked him to give the before-church prayer for the deacons who would be serving communion that day. I can hear my father's stumbling words, refusing, embarrassed and ashamed in a dozen different ways. I am embarrassed for him, for me, for the lack of correspondence between our inner and outer selves.

This history I'm making of my spiritual life cries out for linkages—inner to outer—for interpretation, for understanding, for the bone-piercing unity we think of as salvation. But the more I connect things, the harder it is to keep them in line. The closest most of us can get to unity is metaphor, the face-to-face meeting of unlike things that shakes the walls. The Japanese word for poetry is a combination: *temple* and *words*. How many temple words can I write in a lifetime? How can I bring them on? If I could get my father to the altar, fuming with subversion! If I could sign up for the

Church of Christ, no music but the words. If I could faint with religion, be revived by a woman in a nurse's dress, and faint again; if I could knot and unknot like John Donne, in elegant syllogisms.

Only when all else fails does convergence come. Blessed are the poor in spirit. William James, the great philosopher-theologian, said that in order to reach this state we have to relax, we have to get so exhausted with our struggle that we drop down, give up, and *don't care* any longer. This is precisely the experience of metaphor. Take a simple one from Archibald McLeish, "A poem should be palpable and mute / as a globed fruit." It's a scientific fact that a round fruit is palpable and mute. But beyond that, the mind has to relax to make a different sort of sense. A poem isn't literally palpable except as we touch the page it's printed on. It's mute only in that it can't literally speak from the page. One's attention is diverted from the idea of poem, and from the fruit, and is set free, into the irreducible, inexplicable space between. Anyone can explicate, but finally, a leap of faith is required.

When all else fails: I was about to leave my first husband. I had never been alone before. My grandmother used to say women should go straight from "the protection of their father's house to their husband's," and that's what I did, more or less. Twelve years later, I was standing in our garage-made-into-a-den, with its dismal linoleum floor and braided rug. Overcast sky, dull light through the picture window, mildew growing along the baseboards: a clear signal that the dark and furry world was creeping in, out of my control. I was praying for help. In this way, I rode into the panic until my body gave in to it. For a minute, I combusted into a shower of bliss in my muscles, in my thoughts. I was one with everything. Newton would deny me this, Einstein wouldn't. Quantum mechanics tells us that what we used to think was objective physical reality has proven to be made up of subjective mental constructs. In the progress toward truth, I notice that each step has been from particles to waves, from material to mental.

Einstein understood the slippage in the Word. As have the Episcopal and the Catholic churches, which intend to be "sacramental," not logocentric. One enters the sacred not so much through hearing the Word, but through the holy sacraments, represented by images which are, in essence, metaphors. Metaphor doesn't allow words to mean only what they stand for in the language system. Explanation takes a back seat to understanding. One doesn't reason toward God: one arrives, and in the presence of, say, the Eucharist, or baptism, the sacred arrives also. All yearning ends up here, at the burning bush. We turn aside from the roadway and take off our sandals. Who knows what we encounter? It is what it is.

I became an Episcopalian. Being a child of the story-telling South—and of Dante, Milton, Bunyan, Browning, and

Frost—I see my spiritual life as a narrative, a Pilgrim's Progress. It's an evolution in time, not of my passions, but of my passion, shaped by who I'm becoming, what's needed in the process. No religion, said William James, has ever established or proved itself except by survival of the fittest. My spiritual life is a story of natural selection.

Consider the evolution of our thinking about solid matter, the way matter has recently dissolved in front of our eyes. The closer we've been able to look, the more the vast spaces open up. We can't hold on to anything. The evolution from Word to image to utter abandonment of the referential may be inevitable, if one attends closely enough. Finally, maybe, as D. H. Lawrence said, "It's not religious to be religious." It seemed inevitable for me to finally loosen my allegiance to Christian imagery and begin to practice Buddhist meditation, to learn to pay attention to everything with the greatest possible precision. At the very least, you might say I erased ten centuries of Christianity. The Eastern and Western churches split in the eleventh century over the issue of meditative practice. "Navel-gazers," the Church of Rome called the Eastern Orthodox Church, not understanding (to put the most generous face on it) the profound outward transformation possible in such seemingly self-absorbed practice. Then there were roots in my own church camp prayer-walks, in the silence on the spillway rocks at the end of the singing; in Asian immigration to this country, in an exhaustion of mainstream Christianity's hold on the imagination. In the sixties, there was the Maharishi Yogi, then others. Now there's a young woman sitting in the lotus position on the cover of the J. Crew catalog. And dozens of companies selling zafus, zabutons, bells, and gongs.

Sitting on a cushion is useless. Dancing is useless. Reading or writing a poem is useless. If pressed, most of us will admit that such acts carry a suspicious taint in the deep recesses of our Protestant, Puritan blood. They seem antithetical to Benjamin Franklin, to Thomas Jefferson, to the spirit of the Enlightenment that founded this country. So they are. Oh, there was poetry and dancing in the Bible, in the eighteenth century, and so on. But not the kind that removes you very far from the public sphere, into dangerous private waters. Martin Luther, if he had been born now, might have understood at last, but I'd hate to be the one to try to explain it to him. St. John of the Cross understood. St. Teresa of Avila understood. But they're weird mystics, removed from ordinary life, therefore not dangerous to us. They tell us how, in states of high concentration, metaphor comes to fruition. One thing doesn't simply share abstract aspects of the other. As the theologian Paul Tillich put it, each participates in the reality of the other. Now is forever. Everything is nothing, nothing is everything. I'm you; you're me. This is crazy talk, a private truth, not public. And, unlike Christianity, it even lacks a good plot.

How can humans communicate without a story? Even a lyric poem is an embedded story. Take Keats's "Ode to a

Nightingale": a man feels drugged with the pain in his heart. He hears a bird. He wishes he could sing like that, fade away into the forest with the bird, and forget. Instead, he flies away on the wings of poesy, until the word *forlorn* brings him back. Without linear progression, however artificial, even the senses don't make sense. But the longing of all religion, and of all human endeavor, is to follow that progression to the land of milk and honey, to completion, to peace, to an end to striving.

St. Augustine says three things keep us from that end: time, materiality, and multiplicity. Meister Eckhart, the fourteenth-century preacher and mystic, preached a sermon on this subject:

The fullness of time is when time is no more. . . . In order that fire may catch wood and penetrate it completely, time is required because the wood and the fire are so dissimilar. At first, the fire warms the wood, and then makes it hot, and then smoking and crackling, because the two are so dissimilar, but as the wood gets hotter it gets quieter. The more the wood gives up to the fire, the more peaceful it is, until at last it really turns to fire and time, he says, is no more. This is the way of metaphor. Is the fire now wood? Is the wood now fire? They participate in the meaning of each other.

As for space, Eckhart goes on to say that "when one thing fills another, their boundaries are mutual and in contact with each other and there is no space between." And finally, about multiplicity, he says, "There is no truth that does not include all truth."

I am still in my own story, however, still caught within time, still yearning. I'm in the meditation hall. There's a checkerboard of cushions, mindfully spaced a few inches apart on the wooden floor. I cross my legs to begin an afternoon's sit during which I vow not to move for two hours, no matter what. There is a fly.

The Story of the Fly

There is a fly. Not a very big fly, or a very noisy one, but in the speechless room, it is a menace of wings. I am huge and obvious, the gravity at the center of its universe. It lands, easily, gently, on the cartilage of my ear and at once begins its hairy peregrinations. It can't decide whether to enter the ear or not. It poises on the outer edge. My face, my lower diaphragm, begin to twinge. The excursions of the fly, light as they are, begin to radiate signals to my fingers, my toes. The fly steers into my ear. I am a piece of meat, a damp cavity. The fly will invade my head, burrow out my brain. All I have to do is move, raise my hand and scare the fly away. I am Jesus in the wilderness—all I have to do is say yes to Temptation. I sit. My left foot begins its initial thrumming toward pain, from its unrelieved position. Little by little, I become nothing but suffering. I concentrate on the effects of Fly. I stay with each tiny, hairlike movement, following the reverberations in my body.

My disgust, my aversion, begins to roll like waves of the ocean. This is insane. I'm insane. But there come waves into my insanity like a massage. This goes on for a thousand years, beyond explaining. At last some critical mass of misery, of concentration, is reached, and at that moment, my body simply gives up. It relaxes. The space between Enemy Fly and me collapses. What is invasion? There are no more borders. What is suffering? There's no more suffering, no more clutching. It's not the end of the story, it's all of the story: time and space, expansion and contraction, Alpha and Omega, the Source that breathes out the Word and takes it back.

I made this up because I couldn't resist a story. I wanted a happy ending. It could go this way, certainly, and I'm pretty sure it does go this way. There isn't really an end, actually. The fly and I would be in Nirvana, and then we'd return to live and die in our mundane lives. I'd carry the story with me out of Nirvana, though, like the memory of Eden—that ineffable land where subject and object are one. Sometimes, even in this life, such a place would be possible.

The Back-Ache

The mind is the terriblest force in the world, father,
Because, in chief, it, only, can defend
Against itself. At its mercy, we depend
Upon it.

St. John

The world is presence and not force.
Presence is not mind.
—Wallace Stevens, from "Saint John and the Back-Ache"

There we are at church camp, singing "I love to tell the story, 'twill be my theme in glory, to tell the old, old story . . ." Every time I ask my body to pay strict attention now, it starts to hear the old, old story. Not particularly the Jesus one. The one I hear is older than the past, older than anyone's scripture, so old that time has given up on it and it has become all presence.

Hiking with Amy

There is a little snow on the ground, mostly packed into ice. It takes extra muscles to keep the knees flexed to avoid slipping, and extra concentration to see slick spots. I step in Amy's tracks when I can see them. When I can't, I step in the same spot anyway, secure behind her muscular legs and her nature-woman pigtail thickly flopping to her waist. Not that I'm frail myself. I am a couple inches taller than Amy. I look great for my age, particularly my legs. And I move well. Still, I have to work to keep up. Like the old days, hiking behind my father. He would be silently moving ahead, free as a fox, while the branches and brush tried to trap me in my mother's life. I would point out a blue heron, hoping I had it right. I try to think of something now to say to Amy, to appear nonchalant. She doesn't talk much. She doesn't need to, or she's shy—I haven't been able to figure out which.

"Wow, this is slippery," I say stupidly.

"Sure is," she says.

"Did you know they've added 500 acres to White Clay Creek Park?" I ask.

"That's great," she replies. I try to be funny: "How old do you suppose the elderberries are?" Good grief. I start questioning my need to talk. I wonder about her mother, that phantom I play off against, what she would say or not say, what Amy would think of it. The "real" mother—whatever we imagine her to be—drags love from us whether we can spare it or not. Here I am, the stepmother, arriving too late, after the world has already ended. Add to that the gulf of age that creates its own silence—the past remains untranslatable.

We are taking a three-mile rehearsal hike in the park, trying out our new boots. Amy had informed me that my old ones would end up shredded by the first day of our real hike in the North Cascades next spring, so 1 have bought what she says—a pair of Asolo hiking boots exactly like the ones she's had for eight years. She bought a pair also, to replace those. She bought a can of spray protectant, and sprayed hers, and I used aerosol silicone I found at home on mine. Her spray, though, had beeswax in it, and the suede finish of the shoes got all smashed down, darkened and slick. Her dad and I were sorry for her, her first new pair in so long, but she took them to the shoe repair shop, and the man torched them to make them "breathe" again. But they're still darker and not as pretty. She's a real hiker, though, much more concerned that they work well.

That's what I admire about Amy, her lack of interest in what the world expects. When she graduated from Gettysburg, she moved in with a Domino's driver for a while, then went to Oxford for a year, then backpacked all over Europe by herself. When she needed money, she worked illegally, without a work visa, in a take-out sandwich shop for a few weeks, then went on again. This was when her father and I were getting together, only a few months after her parents' divorce was final. She met me for the first time in Edinburgh, having made bed-and-breakfast reservations for us with no exterior angst. Jerry and I were like a young couple coming to admit to the parents the guilty fact of their love. She had no comment about the new "us." She took us to her favorite pubs, and Jerry and I sat, heavy-lidded, drinking beer, trying to stay awake as late as Amy and her friends.

Then she moved to Pullman, Washington, to get a PhD, but when she finished her MA, she and her new partner Dennis decided to buy a house with a fair amount of land near there in Albion. She's making a little farm like the one she grew up on and still longs for, the one her parents sold because the growing tension between them made the isolation of the country unbearable. She loved that farm. Jerry has memories of her leading a calf around by a leash and sitting between rows of snap peas, eating them warm off the vine. On her new place, she's beefing up the soil and has ordered a lot of plants for spring. She built a table herself, and she's learning how to move interior walls.

Amy and I move naturally at about the same pace on flat ground, but going uphill, I can barely keep up with her. I begin to worry how I'll do, grandmother of four, with a forty-pound pack on my back all day, then another day, and another. I do walk, and I work out at the gym, but these are only predictable drips into the glassy stillness of my days, in front of my computer or a book. And I'm thinking of Proust—the boy reading in his hooded wicker chair until he seems older than his grandmother. The natural world begins to appear to him through filmy cataracts of language. When he picks through, looking for the actual things, they slide away like melting snow, fingers not touching the snow, only the melting edge, the word for it. Likewise, I feel a little awkward; the tangible world retreats from me a step or two.

I am as young as Amy. I am a combination of all of my ages, my present self a scout sent ahead to see what's coming up. My face is starting to fall, the fat pockets in my cheeks migrating downward, drawing faint shadows past my mouth. But unless I'm looking in a mirror, I have to think hard to realize this. I try to think how Amy might perceive me, how my students might, an emissary from that terrible other country. The latest facelift techniques actually move the fat pockets back up where they used to be, instead of just pulling the corners of the face into a Nancy Reagan grin. A facelift doesn't seem as silly as it once did, before I began "enriching" my hair color and taking hormones. Who can draw the line between the naturally occurring and the created? People used to die at forty. My poor mother gave up before she was my age. I still see her eyes, blank brown pools holding her life as still as possible, so it won't hurt so much. It takes a lot to keep moving and stay awake. I'm out here, pitting myself against her to survive, lifting weights at the gym so I won't have her dowager's hump, walking and running, watching my eating so I won't have her stomach. Every day I wake up figuring out how to live.

People used to die at forty surrounded by blood kin. There was hardly time to create families the way we do now, out of the opposite poles of passion and dailiness, instead of out of our own blood. We call them families. In the "unnaturally" long twilight beyond childbearing years, we make our own definitions.

Amy educates me on the other equipment. She says to buy ultradense merino wool socks with thermal regulating fibers and a moisture control system. A sleeping bag must be good for fifteen degrees at least, if I can find one to rent here in Delaware, and must weigh under five pounds. She likes the mummy bags, to keep the body heat in closer. We look at sample bags and tents at I. Goldberg's. I try to pay attention when Amy explains the differences to me, what I should remember, but I am dazzled by the oranges and blues, slick as parachutes. The new stuff is light and warm and packs in a tiny space. I wonder if the technology of hiking has changed the experience of it, if it is better, being light and warm instead of heavy and numb. I wonder what the new miseries are, or if it is just a matter of taking longer to get to the old ones.

After Amy goes back to Washington, I start walking by my-self with the boots on and find that with my heavyweight prescription sports orthotics inside, my toe shoves too hard against the end, going downhill.

I put the boots away in the closet and wear my old cheap ones for the next three months; then I begin to get worried that I won't be able to wear the new ones when the time comes. At last in mid-May, I decide to put my lightweight "dress" orthotics in the new boots, the ones I was using when I bought them. Less support, but they work okay.

The body is held up by the twenty-six small bones of the foot. The arch is supposed to act like a spring to absorb the shock, but my arch is 4-F flat. This causes the astrag-alus bone just above the arch to sink further down, and at the wrong angle, to do its job of bearing the weight of the body from the tibia, the large leg bone. The tibia then drops a fraction lower and off to the side, which causes even the knees to be shoved out of alignment. Orthotics raise and slightly lift the inside of my feet, to distribute the pressure as nearly as possible the way it should have been, if I had never, ever in my life taken off the saddle oxfords I was told to wear by the man who looked at my little-girl bones under the green radiation of the shoe-fitting machine.

Privately, I am glad to keep the new boots stashed in the back of the closet, in favor of my old, easy ones. Part of me wants to stay home with my computer. There we were, visiting Amy last summer, tourists in Washington, walking the brief trails, oohing over the spruces.

"Let's come back next summer; Amy and I can hike," I said, the way people build whole lives in an instant on a mountaintop they've just seen. The unfurling of details began as if my mind were intent on making it so, no matter about me. It was my young mind. I would have been wild to do this at twenty-five, if I hadn't gotten married so early and had babies. I would have loved to live Amy's life. Amy and I are the hikers. Her sister, Pam, although she grew up on the farm, too, is more of a city kid; Jerry has arthritis; and my kids are busy with their own kids. Amy and I are both oldest children, each crushed in the vise of our parents' unhappiness, liking to head out loaded with everything we need across a wilderness that will not bother us if we leave it alone.

At the last minute, late May and early June, I break in my boots. I wear them to the gym. They are heavy and bulky, but I pretend I am a tough mama. I raise the incline on the treadmill until my heels begin to hurt. I could still cancel the whole thing, I say. I put off finding out where to rent equipment. I go out two days before we leave to pick up the tent, backpack, and food. I am impressed by the chemistry of packages of gourmet dried food that heat themselves when you pull a string. I get a lesson in pack adjustment. There are at least a dozen different straps that control how high the pack rides on your hips, how tight it fits against your lower back, and how much you want to cram into it at the top or sides. There is a Velcro adjustment for shoulder width. I learn how to put the tent together. It is easy, but delicate and technical. I am remembering camping and fishing with my first husband and his parents along the White River, sleeping under a pile of old quilts on the rocks, a sheet of plastic around us to keep the dew off. In the morning, the first thing we would see would be mist on the river, trotlines pulled tight. We would set the coffeepot on a grate between two stones. Those were good times, made by ourselves out of nothing. And afterward, they could be made intimate down to the fingertips, pounded into an old Smith Corona typewriter—as opposed to this computer-flicker that barely wants its keys touched.

Days I'm not working out, I walk in the park, mostly the same trail. It is not much different from the gym—the predictable, lone disciplinary pleasure, the iamb: one-two, one-two, one foot on the ground at all times, the heartbeat of it, while I watch the trail for stones or roots, think about, say, dinner, and at the same time notice tight coils of ferns breaking through and identify individual trees by their bark. I don't say their names, but they're there, part of my past, keeping me company in some layer of consciousness, all the same—the ragged bark of the persimmon, the hawthorne, the ash, the rivulets of bark on the pin oak, and the smoother, stippled skin of the alder and the birch. I am moving like wildfire compared to them, through violets and spring beauties, through cathedrals where trees crowd out the undergrowth, through mud holes where boot prints and hoof prints have concocted a black mush. I like the science of finding a way around obstacles without breaking my stride. Determining what to step on, whether the advantage is in the middle or off to the side.

My right foot alone is a scientific wonder. Two years ago, the podiatrist sawed through my first metatarsus and repositioned the pieces to reestablish a comfortable notch for the tendon that had been pressing miserably against the ground. I also now use cushioning liners—the thin green ones that absorb an amazing amount of impact—and then I have the orthotics, all of which I have to transfer from shoe to shoe every time I change. I always know my feet are there—something always hurts a little. The podiatrist has added a cushion to protect my second toe from impact. He also suggests knee braces, for the hike.

I have rented the pack and sleeping bag and gotten together the things Amy has listed for me. I have the athletic braces with holes cut out for the knees, the gel blister bandages, the drinking cup, the Off for deep woods, three days' underwear plus one, two short-sleeved shirts, one long, one thermal jacket, tights to sleep in, D-cell batteries, flashlight, food packs, and sticks that glow in the dark when you bend them in the middle. I have these things lined up on the hearth, with my list, so as not to forget anything. It is like writing a poem—each object stands for a great deal; you don't want to leave anything out. You have to pack them all in the smallest space possible, because you have to carry them. You dream of the evening when you set up camp, the aaaah, when things come together, when you've made yourself a little community in the middle of nowhere.

We sign in at the Wolf Creek trailhead, saying how many of us are hiking and how long we will be gone, in case. I wonder how often these boxes get checked. Briefly, I think of the Misfit in "A Good Man Is Hard to Find," shooting the whole family, one by one—and they had only driven down a side road, not deep into woods. It is a surprise that the full pack balances and hugs my back so closely that I feel no strain, only weight. Amy's carrying twenty pounds more than I am, not complaining. I take the rear, lost in that initial dream in which nothing hurts and the woods break away to each side, new and green, and Wolf Creek roars to one side, newly vocal. Within an hour, one of my boot laces—which I should have double-tied—comes loose and catches on a hook of the other boot, and I fall hard, pack pulling me over sideways, feet locked together like a prisoner's. My head and knees are bleeding. I struggle to get up, glancing into the ravine where my limp and broken doppelganger lies outstretched on a rock. Amy digs out her red first aid kit calmly; maybe she doesn't want to scare me. "Does it hurt much?" she asks. "No, I'm fine," I say, not knowing if it's true or not.

Soon I am able to go on, my body a little quivery, the path more intractable, my mind more subdued.

No one has cleared the trail this spring because of the snow. The Cascades have had twice as much snow as usual and a cool spring, which means slower melt. We climb over fallen logs so huge that we have to remove our packs, inch over the top, hand the packs across and put them on again on the other side. Streams that should have been barely passable are exploding with water. It pours over the tops of our good waterproof boots as we wade across. My socks and liners act like sponges, each step a small, cold lake, sloshing onward and upward.

Fatigue begins to show up in me as clumsiness. I bump a rock and stagger a little. "You're stuck with me now, no matter what," I tell Amy. She says she's had far worse companions. "You knew enough to be nervous ahead of time," she says. "Once I had to carry most of a friend's pack half the way back, with her complaining all the time." It's hard to figure what holds us to each other, I think.

We start looking for a place to camp, but it is another hour before we find a place wide and flat enough to suit Amy. By this time, my feet are robotic, no longer interested in the rest of my body. The clearing is on a slight slope—not great for sleeping, but near water and clear of brush. It has an old fire pit and a nail in a tree. "Good enough," Amy says, looking it over as if she were buying a used car. "Other people didn't want to go any farther, either." She blows stray hairs out of her face, tired but focused. We study the pale green concentric circles on the topographical map. I pretend to be able to pay attention while she locates where we are. She thinks we have climbed about two thousand feet.

"Fire starter," Amy calls me, and I call her "Trash woman." She is in charge of hanging everything with any odor to it—even our toothpaste—ten feet high and five feet from a tree trunk at night, to keep them away from animals and keep animals away from us. I build good fires. I was well-taught, but now I half-cheat, using half a tiny fire-starter log. I am a thousand years old, crouched over my teepee of twigs; I am my father. No, I have no gender, no name, my eyes are all fire. Gradually, I add larger and larger sticks, mesmerized, utterly devoted. The wood is wet, and we get a lot of smoke and popping. We try both the Vegetable and Rice Medley and the Beef Stew. The rice is much better—the potatoes in the stew don't hydrate completely. They come out chewy squares, like new bubble gum.

We've seen no other person all day. No one, most likely, is within ten miles of us in any direction. Considering the hikers recently shot in Yellowstone, the fact ought to be comforting, but the mind longs for company. It goes on as it has learned to do over the years, inventing cars and people walking on the far side of the path, beyond the evergreens. A distant waterfall could just as easily be a freeway. The forest is stunningly silent on the matter of metaphor. Deer raise their heads, show the whites of their tails, and walk farther uphill behind a clump of trees, as if to say, "So what?" That's what I keep hearing as I think my thoughts, as I store up what I want to write later. Amy sets her shoes on a rock to dry and scrubs the inside of the coffeepot, as if the shoes, the rock, the coffeepot, were not floating in the insubstantial radiance of the universe, of the same substance as my thoughts.

Humans have known for a long time that there is really no reason to think of matter as solid. Joseph Priestley showed this in the eighteenth century, long before quantum physics. He discovered oxygen, which filled in the void where before only heavenly ether lived. He wrote a book called *History of Electricity*, tracing the measurable impulse through thin air to its measurable conclusion. What we call our individual consciousness, most likely, is entirely physical, a force field, arranged in a somewhat different way from the force field of the rock or the deer or another person. Nevertheless, a mule deer wanders into camp, sniffing the trash bag while we watch, its body lean and wild, ready to bolt—a follower of Proust, I think, certain that staying alive means keeping separate, endlessly picking through the details.

We take only our day packs today for the climb to the top of the trail. A quarter mile past our camp, we find the ideal camping spot, flat, right next to a waterfall, cut log seats placed comfortably around a fire pit. We sit awhile watching water pour around fallen trees, the vision of what we might have had holding us longer than we meant.

Increasingly as we walk, there are patches of dense old snow. Sometimes we can stand on the surface, but usually we leave deep prints. We are on a movie set now, wading through snow with our shorts on, sweating from the work of it. To either side, tiny pink flowers change to blue, or vice versa, on the same stem. I try to figure out which is older. The flower does not exist in my guidebook. In the clearings, grass is intensely green. Higher still, we walk through silver ghosts of trees, an old fire, which allows us to see more easily the snowy peaks, luminescent in occasional sun. We are in the middle of the scene we had witnessed from below, staring right into Abernathy Ridge, peaks all around, rising behind the brittle trunks as if another planet were coming up over the horizon. Then the path narrows to nothing in Gardner Meadow, the end of the trail according to the map, 5,700 feet, marked here by a small bench. There is a lot of snow, and lilies, in the damp soil of its withdrawal. I find in my book the name for the tiny Glacier Lily, opening like a yellow knife and then bending its swan-head slightly. And the rare Calypso, or Deer-head orchid, the most hidden, the most delicate of woodland flowers, spiked purple petals flaring from its cupped base. I like looking at the ground, surrounded by this expanse, and saying these names.

I have tried to ignore my hurting knees as much as possible: Complaining won't help, and there's nothing Amy could do about it anyway. But as we start downhill, they swell and collect fluid and begin to throb. Every step downward jabs at my tibia bones. I try to compensate. I get myself a walking stick, trading iambs for anapests. I pack snow in-side my knee-braces. I try to meditate inward through the pain. Shinzen, my meditation teacher, says that the real test of how skillful you've become is the intensity of sen-sations you can let pass through you without locking your mind and your muscles down on them, congealing them, distorting reality. After ten years, I am still a beginner, hurt-ing like hell.

> There is a pain—so utter—
> It swallows substance up—
> Then covers the Abyss with Trance—
> So Memory can step
> Around—across—upon it—
> As one within a Swoon—
> Goes safely—where an open eye—
> Would drop Him—Bone by Bone.

I don't say Dickinson's poem, of course, but I have learned it before, so it is somewhere inside me, doing its work. Inside the miraculous concentration of her poems, each instant is separated into its individual threads. Each stream of physi-cal sensation, each picture quickly flashing on the interior screen, each thought, each memory as it dashes through and sinks to nothing—is meticulously separated and laid out in the sun, glistening with the moisture of its arrival. It is a pleasure. To open the eyes—to lose concentration—would tangle the threads into the abstraction called pain.

I am ten years old. My stomach is wrenched in pain. My mother is making the bed, crying. A postcard has come for my father from some woman he knew when he was stationed in the Philippines; I hear this when I am older. At the time, there is only the white snap of the sheets and my stomach, aware beyond itself—these two sensations bonded into one suffering it will take years to separate.

I concentrate on keeping on, one step, one step, into the brink, into the next, not toward home but toward the next step. I do not look up, do not notice the scenery. When I stop, there it is, all the same, a series of photographs. I wouldn't have not come. Amy lags behind, taking pictures now that we're on the way back. I am aware that I'll never be able to do this again. Every step, only this once. I have to look down, to place each foot between rocks, between ledge and outcropping, between shale and shale. In the dim part of my brain that goes on living its own life, no matter what, I am thinking, "This, for sure, is not thinking, but walking, perfectly walking." I do think of the end of "A Good Man Is Hard to Find," when the Misfit shoots the grandmother and says, "She would have been a good woman, if it had been somebody there to shoot her every minute of her life."

What if the pain causes me to lose my balance on a ledge? Balance is all in the knees. Not to ask what if, but simply to go on, not thinking, not doing anything but moving on, the mind saying Go On as its own personal grace, the body staying with the task until it is over the hump, by itself.

It is the second night in camp, after the climb down from the peak. My knees give, and I am falling, pitching and turning in my bedroll. Everyone will be sorry I am gone, I think without emotion, as if I were already past that. I catch an updraft; it is good to have back the old dream of flying. I am molecular, carried on drifts like a Chagall figure, nobody's pain hurting me, not even my own. This sequence happens over and over, as if I am trying to figure out how to do it, or if I really want to leave so much behind.

Not that it matters. The next day I am awkwardly attached to the earth again, but it is an earth growing ever more merciful, sloping more gently as we descend. Near the trailhead, cows are grazing in our path and in the woods. Amy is back on the farm, hooting them out of the way. They move back, big-eyed and docile, glad to be a part of the common endeavor of noise and flutter. I am feeling slow-witted as a cow, although Jerry tells me they aren't stupid. I am all cow, my eyes and ears watchful, but my mind—inextricably a part of my tired body—is tired. Amy fills the water jugs for the last time while I sit on a log, vaguely thinking I should help, otherwise thinking nothing.

When we get back to Albion, Amy is more talkative. She likes showing me what she's done. She is making the old gardens flourish and has made new ones on each side of the house. She has dug out overgrown shrubs and trees, planted rows of snap peas, green beans, tomatoes, roses, creeping thyme, strawberries, blackberries, an amazing start. She has bought a circular saw, a router, a band saw. She has reroofed the garage. She identifies the plants I'm not sure of, tells me what the saws are for, the different blades. We speak in exactitudes I know by heart. I am watching my father saw boat planks. He is chewing his tongue to get it right. I want to belong to him, so I ask the names of things. The names, the actions, separate love, fear, anger, and regret into workable portions of some unity we can only imagine. One goes safely "within a swoon," as Dickinson says of the words themselves. To the west, the Cascades go on rising, crumbling to plains, reforming—a great, regular breathing out of which details drift upward like hot sparks. The Dacron tent like a kite at full sail, its tiny fiberglass poles strung together on an elastic band, the one-pot Coleman stove, the blue bedroll light and sleek as a feather—these I will hate to return; they are so clever, so young and shapely.

New Car

In 1886, Gottlieb Daimler fitted a horse carriage with his four-stroke engine. In 1889, he built two vehicles from scratch, with several innovations. From 1890 to 1895 he and his assistant built about thirty vehicles, either at the Daimler works or in the Hotel Hermann, where he set up shop after falling out with his backers.

I'm thinking of trading this car. I say *trade* because it sounds more responsible than the real truth, which is that I just plain *want a new one*. This is how most of us are. No matter that we've been climbing in and out of the same car for years, running it through touchless car washes, making it our home on long trips, piling boxes in the trunk. No matter that we know it and it knows us. That we know the exact speed, the feeling of the gas pedal, when it always begins to make that peculiar noise. When the urge comes upon us, we begin to create the litany of reasons why we should move on. We consult our mechanic, who says, "Well, you need new tires, which will cost you $550, and you need to have the brakes relined, a new catalytic converter . . ."

In 1879, George Baldwin Selden of Rochester, New York, applied for
a patent for the first American car with a gasoline internal com-
bustion engine. Selden did not build a model until 1905, when he
was forced to do so owing to a lawsuit threatening the legality of
his patent because the subject had never been built. Selden later
sued the Ford Motor Company for infringing on his patent. Selden's
case against Ford went all the way to the Supreme Court, which
ruled that Ford, and anyone else, was free to build automobiles
without paying royalties to Selden, since automobile technology
had improved so significantly since the design of Selden's patent
that no one was building according to his early designs.

We add it up. At some magical total, we'll declare the car
isn't worth it, although in our heart of hearts we know that,
unlike with people, we could keep replacing parts almost
forever. The cost of replacements would never amount to
the payments for a new car, but we don't say that to ourselves. We want the tight seals, the clean upholstery, the
new dashboard—especially the dashboard. One day we stop
by a car dealership. We didn't even know we were going
to stop. It feels a little like cheating. We stroll through, we
eye the dazzling dashboards, and our soul takes off, lights
blinking, OnStar beaming only to us.

As with marriages. I know. If they're breaking down, we pay
the cost, daily, and one ordinary day just like every other,
we say "that's enough." People always want to know what
made us leave, but we know there's no one problem, no one
difficulty of personality. But we can clearly remember the

moment when our souls turned a corner. Most of us can recall where we were, what we were doing. We tried to put it
off, tried to pretend to ourselves we could go on. But while
we were bending to pick up a shirt to toss into the dirty
clothes, or rinsing a plate at the sink, exactly then, the body
itself decided to speak to us, to save us.

*Since the 1920s nearly all cars have been mass-produced, so mar-
keting plans have heavily influenced automobile design. It was Al-
fred P. Sloan who established the idea of different makes of cars
produced by one firm, so that buyers could "move up" as their
fortunes improved. The makes shared parts with one another so
that the larger production volume resulted in lower costs for each
price range.*

I'm sitting in a lawn chair on the patio I personally built. I'm
pretending to read. Dennis has just gotten out of bed. He
opens the sliding door and stands half-in, half-out, blinking
in the sunlight. He's wearing a crumpled white shirt, tail out.
Sun on the shirt is all I see. "I'm going to leave. I'm going to
get an apartment," I say, my words steaming upward from
some small fissure, the pressure of years behind them. As
I speak, I know what I say is true, exactly, that I will leave,
and at once. That the words have been true for years, and
now suddenly shape themselves in the outer world.

That's long past. Right now I'm remembering the car I drove
off in, the two-year-old tan Subaru I'd bought just weeks
before.

The 2007 Subaru Legacy 2.5i Limited sedan pricing starts at $24,095, plus $625 delivery fee. A 1988 Subaru dl, four-wheel drive is available locally for $440.

I'm thinking of all the past cars, the new ones, the sold and abandoned ones, the, well, shifting of gears, they represented. I'm thinking about these cars while heading contentedly enough down New London Road toward Superfresh in this '95 Honda Accord, my hard-working vehicle that no one would ever accuse of representing anything very dramatic. It's eleven years old and doing fine, as long as I can tolerate the roar at certain speeds caused by a flawed exhaust system design. You should picture me in it, because it might give you an idea of me. I like it because it's pretty much invisible: it's a car, it runs. I bought it used, a year old, with scratches on the hood where obviously someone had tried to clean off spilled wiper fluid with abrasives. I made a quick attempt to polish off the scratches, then forgot about them except to use to them to spot my car in the parking lot among the other champagne gold Honda Accords.

A 1997 Accord is the oldest listed today on the Internet, for $15,900. There is no local listing for a car this old. Kelley Blue Book gives the Accord Hybrid its Best Resale Value Award in the sedan category. The award honors vehicles that are expected to have the best resale value after five years of ownership.

A person picks out a car from such a vast array of possibilities; every one must stand for something. Like a marriage: what does it mean that this is the choice I made? Who am I, who would ride in this? Who am I, who used to ride in that?

The first car I remember is the Buick sitting in the driveway between my two sets of grandparents' houses. I'm six or seven. We're living in the Browns' house, my father's parents, while they're away. The car is a midnight blue, its paint oxidized to a ragged dullness. It's very old even then. I think of it as standing for my father, a sleek-lined, dark obstinacy parked right where my other grandparents have to look at it when they turn into their driveway in their new-every-few-years DeSoto. I don't remember riding in the Buick. But I love the name: plosive, spit out like a taunt to the soft-vowelled DeSoto.

Why did Granddaddy Simpich give us the DeSoto? What's the symbolism of parents giving large gifts to their children? Do we do it to make them happy? So they won't suffer? To prove we still have the upper hand? To shame our not-quite-adequate sons- or daughters-in-law? I don't know. The year cars sprouted tail fins as if the road were a launching pad, Granddaddy gave us his 1949 DeSoto: gray, rounded like a small elephant, its front grill a chronic toothy chrome smile. I remember, and I've felt many times since, the joy mixed with sadness, guilt, and unease.

Walter P. Chrysler introduced DeSoto in the summer of 1928. In the first year, DeSoto built more cars than Chrysler, Pontiac, or

Graham-Paige. The record stood for nearly thirty years. The car name honored Hernando de Soto, the sixteenth-century Spaniard who discovered the Mississippi River and had covered more North American territory than any other early explorer. The name De-Soto reinforced the Americana theme sounded by Chrysler's other new brand, Plymouth.

I take in the clean smell of the good upholstery, the broad, flat gaze of windshield. The tension of my father's angry acceptance, his grudging gratefulness couched in his usual disclaimer: "I don't know how he thinks he can just give away a car. It's crazy." Read: people should take care of themselves, it's shameful not to, and, by implication, foolish and shameful to give things away, because you might not be able to take care of yourself later. This philosophy has played out lately in his determination to live on little more than Social Security and his state pension, while socking away thousands and thousands. He drives an '86 Dodge Caravan that my mother made him buy (used) before she died.

It's strange. Sometimes I drive along at a good clip, and the faces I pass seem to see me more clearly than I see myself. They are like the old man and woman who appear to sit all day on the porch of the farmhouse down the road in Kemblesville. They seem like ideal parents, ruminating on the passing of things, on the folly of believing there's somewhere to get to, some need to represent myself a certain way. I've become the unknown, the unknowable, passing in front of their eyes, and they go on sitting, reading their newspaper or just sitting, unconcerned.

The 1949 DeSoto had a feature called "Fluid Drive." To get under-way, one used the clutch to shift the gear lever into "high." Then, one merely pressed the accelerator. If conditions permitted, one eased the foot from the gas around fourteen miles per hour, al-lowing Simplimatic to shift from third to fourth gear. Coming to a light, Simplimatic shifted back down independently. The fluid drive coupling made sure there was no stalling and no need to clutch. As DeSoto stressed, the operation could be performed hundreds of times with a minimum of effort.

My grandparents said they gave us the DeSoto because we were moving from Missouri to Arkansas, and they wor-ried about our old car. The DeSoto was five years old at that time; I was in the fourth grade. The move was terrible for me in ways I only understood later. I was the oldest, I could see that my parents could barely cope with the world, and without my grandparents, I was elected to be in charge. You can see it in my eyes, serious, hooded, straight-on in the pictures. I remember the car loaded with suitcases, boxes, blankets, on our way to Fayetteville. And I remember it many other times as a little house that contained us all, my par-ents, my sister, my retarded brother, our cats, and later my youngest sister. It felt good, actually, to be crowded in, all together, even with the tensions, the fighting, the sulking, and so on. This is the way it is with children. They prefer the collect of family to anything, no matter how difficult. They understand it rightly as the garden they're growing in. To be uprooted from it seems far worse than putting up with weeds, broken bottles, cans, and poor soil.

The DeSoto's talking points were roomy interiors with chair-high seats and a smooth ride. One advertisement showed an enthusiastic DeSoto passenger asking the proud driver, "New road?" The driver replied, "No, new DeSoto!"

In the fifties, when we were headed down the highway toward Arkansas, the American car was being exploited for the first time by advertisers as a symbol for more than simply wealth and convenience. The new ones had turned into rockets, arrayed with gadgets. You could cut out of there and "See the U.S.A. in your Chevrolet." Cars were traveling cafés, cocoons for watching movies at the drive-in. With their bench seats, they were sofas for making out—two sofas actually, one for friends in the back. It was a big deal when the new cars arrived each year, the more upswept fins, the accumulating fillips of chrome, the curving windshields. Many people bought a new one every year or so. But my family, through most of my childhood and adolescence, was stuck in 1949. For as my father frequently said, about the car and everything else, we could never afford to replace it.

For a few years, of course, our car wasn't that much older than others. We enjoyed a normalcy that I would have appreciated more later. Children don't think about status unless their parents do, and mine didn't seem to notice the myriad ways in which they were different from the rest of the world. Except my mother would speak reverently of her parents' new car, but in a tone one might use of St. Paul's Cathedral—a beauty entirely out of reach. The car was, after all, just a way to get to the store, the park, the creek. Mother didn't drive, and liked to be taken on rides, and so it was a way to see places outside of the ordinary routes, dirt roads at that time, just outside of town. And to get to the airport, to watch planes take off. And to A&W root beer, if we were lucky.

By the time I was thirteen, the DeSoto had morphed into a monstrous toad, an oxidized embarrassment with frayed seat covers, a symbol of a family unlike Others, one that Didn't Fit In. My father would pick up my friends and me at the movies. "God, this old car," I would say, rolling my eyes to let my friends know that I Knew it was not okay. Once, my father leaned back and said, "You think your friends are too highfalutin' to ride in this car?" *Highfalutin'*, oh, it cut me to the core, such a deliberately crude word, crude thought, a rebuke I couldn't fight back from, huddled hopelessly with my friends in the back seat. Once—thank heaven—I began to drive by myself, three days after my sixteenth birthday, I could make a joke of the car. I could take it out and drive it fast out by the Agri farm, to show I was cool, no matter what. I'd shift into second, third, then I'd hear and feel the little thump as the Fluid Drive shifted into fourth. I was over the hump, escaped from my father, my mother, my brother, my sister, my messy life on Maxwell Drive. From dirty diapers, tears, peat pots, screwdrivers, and armatures of motors piled everywhere in what was supposed to be a den.

The DeSoto turned over 100,000 miles in 1964, in Cape Girardeau, Missouri, before my father gave up on it. By that time, I was married and had moved back to Arkansas. For those many years, though, it stood for my family, its failure to fit in, the embarrassment of it. Is it possible that one of the reasons I married at seventeen was Harry's parents' two-tone '58 Buick station wagon? Although his parents ran a donut shop and my father was a college professor, although we had almost nothing in common but lust, Harry did have that Buick to drive. It's amazing to me, the way we attach ourselves to symbols, half expecting them to save us.

There were two versions of the 1958 Buick Special Estate Wagon, the pillared four door and the four-door hardtop style. The hardtop style station wagon was available in both the Special and Century trim levels. Estate Wagons were big flashy cars with bright work and chrome, easily identified.

What did the Buick Wagon mean? It was a ship on wheels, wide and deep. It rolled along, solidity itself, in the ocean of my confused world. It meant ordinary family, the kind with a golden retriever flopping its ears out the window. It was new enough to signal a paid-up membership in the club of those who buy things before their old ones get shabby, who don't agonize and rave about every purchase, who plan and agree upon and actually enjoy rather than suffer their acquisitions. I could slide across the seat to elegantly tap my cigarette in the ashtray, a thousand miles from my native land.

A gas cap that will fit the 1958 Buick Station Wagon is available on eBay for forty-five dollars.

The first car Harry and I picked for ourselves was a '62 Volkswagen. Oh joy, it was new. It was new, blue, tidy, and foreign. It was the car of the newly hatching hippies, as well as of smart-minded young adults. To me, its size was its virtue. No room for family, yet. I was utterly and finally free. I've always liked camping out, the way it reduces complications to the size of a tent. The Beetle was a pup tent of a car with poor ventilation, a heater that depended on the motor's being white hot to generate any heat at all, and so noisy that you felt no separation from your environment. You were the road and the road was you, only inches under your feet, roaring through your ears, vibrating your hands on the wheel. No flowers in a tiny vase on the dashboard, like the newer replicas. Just pure functionality: a car. It ran. And it could wiggle out of any space.

Adolf Hitler was searching for a people's car that was capable of transporting three children and two adults at speeds of sixty miles per hour. The car was to be inexpensive, costing the same as a motorcycle. The Volkswagen Beetle first came on the scene in 1947, but they were known by a different name, KdF, short for Kraft durch Freude, meaning "power by joy." In English, the name Beetle was used. In German, they were known as Kafer, and in French they were called Coccinelle.

When we finally traded for a cushy Buick Skylark, I cried. But we had Kelly by then, another child on the way, and supposedly needed a bigger car. How could I ever be young again? Skylark: how ironic. How could I ever fly out of this terrible marriage? Kelly, who was four at the time, threw up over and over because of the new car's soft springs hwuumph-hwuumphing us over the Ozark mountains.

The Skylark commemorated Buick's fiftieth anniversary. Built as a limited edition, it was at first available only as a convertible. The body design made it look lower and sleeker than a standard convertible. The windshield was laid over, and the wheel wells were opened up considerably. A body-length strip swept from the front fender down to the front base of the rear wheel well, then outlined the front of the wheel well before ending at the taillights.

In 1968, the Skylark received a new, top-of-the-line 350 cid v8. Known as the L77, this engine had a four-barrel carb, 10.25:1 compression ratio, and was rated at an impressive 280 bhp and a whopping 375 lb-ft of torque.

The Skylark threatened to run itself out from under you if you gave it too much gas. Two years after we bought it, Harry, who was district engineer for the Arkansas Highway Department, was transferred to Huntsville, thirty miles away. We moved, but my heart and my friends remained in Fayetteville. My marriage had hollowed out to a deep loneliness, but I wasn't willing to say so, even to myself. I was exiled. I took Kelly to nursery school in Fayetteville three days a week. If I were heading back alone, I drove that Skylark like a maniac over the country roads, acting out the desperation in my heart.

To follow the fate of the Skylark is to follow my own. Not long after I divorced Harry, I married Dennis. This hasty marriage was doomed from the beginning, but I preferred to gradually go numb for twelve years, for reasons that seemed entirely plausible at the time. The first year, when I was still teaching high school, the ratcheting up of the intensity of my life, the attempt to hold a gorgeous goateed madman in my domestic arms, made me absentminded. Carpooling my group to school in the Skylark, I pulled out in front of a Karmann Ghia in the rain. There were a few bruises and the car was pretty much wrecked, but since Dennis and I had decided to both finish graduate school together, we had no money for a replacement. I found someone willing to patch up the car. The hood wouldn't stay down, so he used those bolts that stick up through the hood and go through a pin, like on racing cars. Embarrassing.

Talk about embarrassing: Dennis, who grew up poor-white-trash poor, came equipped with a 1970 blue Ford Mustang with two wide black racing stripes down the hood. He had bought it new and, like a man born on another planet and not understanding the complicated gradations of this one, thought it was beautiful. He called it "LeRoy." Probably one of the reasons I fell in love with him is that he had a car named LeRoy. Naming the hunk of steel that gets you around, well, the world becomes animate, full of playful spirits. It was only the name I liked. Its stripes embarrassed me, oh terribly, especially after the Skylark died and for a while I had to drive the kids and me to church in LeRoy. But I had long ago learned to park in an obscure part of a lot, blank out when people noticed me behind the wheel, and compensate by holding myself to wildly unreasonable standards of excellence in every other way.

Available in 1969 and 1970 only, the small "boss 429" decal on each front fender hinted at a very special Mustang. Holding a big block with a huge bore and hemispherical combustion chambers, the motor had staggering potential for power. The brainchild of the late Larry Shinoda, the car as finished product was disappointing to him. He was quoted as saying he had wanted a ten-second-capable car in factory form. The actual car wasn't up to such wild times. It had a rev limiter, a restrictive intake manifold and exhaust. And all of the smog equipment choked it down. The finished product was still strong, but neither an automatic transmission

nor air conditioning was available. In the case of the latter, there
simply wasn't enough room under the hood.

We all adapted by developing a family allegiance to LeRoy
that amounted to the allegiance to Dennis—we celebrated
its in-your-face uncouthness as best we could. Dennis said
it was the best car ever made, and so the kids and I agreed.
Not to agree was to risk opening the deep suitcase of anger,
disappointment, and loneliness we carried with us.

The Skylark died because its block burst in the cold. I'll
bet it was my fault. At that time, I wasn't any good at taking care of cars. I think it didn't have enough antifreeze in
it. Or maybe it didn't have any. I was taking classes, trying
to get my PhD, worrying about grocery money. The man at
the Mobil station got me in touch with a little old lady, literally, who had a very old tan Chevy (I forget what model
or year) that she couldn't drive any more. When I test drove
it, it coasted down the hill into a ditch only a few feet from
Old Wire Road's steady traffic. The brake fluid had dried
up. That solved, I bought it for $250. But when we left Fay-
etteville for Delaware, we left it behind. The trip seemed
too far for it. We headed for Delaware with me driving Le-
Roy and Dennis trying to wrestle a huge Ryder truck over
the mountains.

Although the Mustang handled better than most of its muscle
car peers, some fine-tuning was still needed. Most notable was

staggering the rear shock absorbers to prevent wheel hop. Heavier spring rates, wider tires, and subtly flared wheel arches also helped. To make a distinctive visual impact, there was a C-stripe side appliqué and rear window slats. To aid aerodynamics, a front chin spoiler and trunk-mounted rear wing were added. The look was so well received that by the start of 1970 production, the window slats and spoilers were offered as an option on all Mustang fastbacks. A 1970 Mustang with engine rebuilt in 1988, driven rarely since, was sold on eBay Motors in 2002 for $29,999.99.

Imagine us driving into Newark, Delaware, in LeRoy. Our fellow faculty members, many of them with Ivy League degrees, had family money and gorgeous old highboys passed down through generations. We had LeRoy. For the first year, we were given, at a low rent, a dignified faculty house right across Orchard Road from the university president. LeRoy wouldn't start in the cold, and there we were, all four of us, pushing him down the road in the snow to get him started. There we were, invited to dinner at a faculty member's house in fashionable old Wawaset Park, driving up and down the street in LeRoy, looking for the house until our host had to come out and flag us down, racing stripes and all.

That was 1978. I sat in a corner of the bedroom and studied for my PhD exams. Public school teachers went on strike for three months, and so the kids were hanging around the house, lonely and bored. Dennis was more erratic than ever, wracked with anxiety about "making it" in this *highfalutin'* place. Ah, the word itself traps its user in a constructed, symbolic world! The word comes attached to some image—a house in Wawaset Park, a pair of Princeton khaki pants, an ancient oriental rug. As the mind grasps the image, it elevates it to symbolic significance. An image-shaped door is flung open into a violent, wordless world made up of what we want, or what we don't want. Desire and disgust travel through the body in waves, the tug of war between what might be (vague) and what is (equally vague, obscured with the fog and trinkets of the mind). The world the door opens into is what we call the heart, the symbolic heart, which stands for the invisible junction of mind and body. The heart in turn is symbolized by a flat valentine, the dip in the middle standing for its two lobes, two lovers, and the entry and exit of connection.

Although my heart took its time in announcing to me that it was time to leave Dennis, my mind did make sure I bought the tan Subaru sedan several weeks ahead. I bequeathed him the little blue Subaru station wagon, the car I'd also picked out, that he'd finally been willing to trade LeRoy for. By this time, the station wagon had rust on its fenders, patched with fiberglass goo and repainted so that it looked pretty good, but the car, I knew, was close to being finished. Good enough for him, I thought. He'd insisted on staying in the house I'd provided the down payment for, out of my retirement money from high school teaching.

Subaru is a Japanese word meaning unite, as well as a term iden-
tifying a cluster of seven stars, which the Greeks called the Pleia-
des—part of the Taurus constellation. According to Greek mythol-
ogy, Atlas's daughters turned into this group of stars. In 1953, five
Japanese companies merged to form Fuji Heavy Industries Ltd. The
new corporation adopted the "Subaru" cluster of stars as the official logo for its line of automobiles.

Back to the fiberglass goo, the memory of which makes me
cringe. It stands for my life—staring off at the stars, unwill-
ing to confront, to make a scene, trying to believe I'm being
a good person even when I'm being royally had, and am furious. One day a couple of guys cruised down our modest
subdivision street, looking for rust on cars. They came to the
door. We were living hand to mouth on Dennis's assistant
professor's salary and my part-time teaching. Okay, I said.
For sixty dollars, we could be rid of the rust. The car might
last longer. One guy drove off and the other got to work.
He sanded a little, and smeared the white paste around,
and called it done. I thought he'd paint, but no, he'd just
agreed to fix it. He wanted cash. "How much again?" I asked.
"Sixty, or whatever you think it's worth," he said. I could
have sent him on his way with nothing, but I drove to the
shopping center to get sixty dollars cash. Then he needed
a ride home. I drove him home. Good grief.

Sometimes you're told what stands for what. Even if you're
not, if you keep finding wrens, red scarves, or footlockers

in a novel, you begin to suspect that they're symbolic in some way or other. It's obsession that gives an object its power: car as marriage, or car as personality, or car as witness. But the thing about the object of attention is that it remains an object, no matter what we make it into. Eventually a car gets hauled off to the crusher, and by that time, we're somewhere else, out of that narrative. Maybe we're someone else. Maybe we've changed a lot. I have.

My next car will probably be a Civic hybrid. That small environmental symbol in our country's vast cesspool of waste. This is what I think about on my way to Superfresh. The sky's clear. White Clay Creek Park looms up to the left of me, its old evergreens partially shading the road. The slow earth can't keep up with the human race. Frogs and wolves are dwindling. Are they suffering in their gradual attrition? I don't think so. They each live their unseen lives satisfied in their way. They don't know they're canaries in the mine. The mental leap that connects frog and canary is too much for frogs. But one day, the earth will speak for them, and say, "That's enough," and save itself. I hope so.

A jury of forty-six international automotive journalists selected the 2006 Civic Hybrid, which achieves an EPA-estimated city/highway fuel economy of 49/51 miles per gallon, as the winner of the 2006 World Green Car. The most economical and environmentally responsible gasoline-powered Civic ever, the 2006 Civic Hybrid is equipped with a continuously variable transmission (CVT) as standard equipment. *The* cvt *allows it to deactivate all four of its cylinders and operate using only the electric motor in certain steady-state cruising situations. Compared to the 2006 Civic Sedan with an automatic transmission, the Civic Hybrid provides a city fuel-economy increase of approximately 63 percent and a highway fuel-economy increase of 27 percent.*

The Subaru sedan I drove off in when I left Dennis broke down twice in the first year. Also, right after I moved into the apartment with my son Scott (who, by the way, had to start college the very next day), he took the car one night and a drunk student crashed through the windshield on her bike. Poor Scott came home white and trembling, his whole life broken to pieces again. But once I got the car fixed, it ran great for the next ten years, well into my third—happy—marriage, well into my children's marriages.

I let that car, and this Honda, stand for this good life. But of course one of those cars is gone, and this one's days are numbered. A symbol is like an exoskeleton, like chrome or steel: useful while you're inside it. It feels safe: you have things figured out, this equals that. You take hold of a symbol and drive along, not thinking exactly, but letting thoughts flash up, images pass away. But each time you step out of it, it seems as if you've just been born into the inescapably dying world. You've been guilty of hiding things, including your complicated self. The equation you constructed wasn't quite the right one anyway. The story of your passing along is like water in your hands. When you turn around, if you decide to, the route becomes entirely strange, everything reversed, backsides showing, which proves that nothing is reliable but motion itself.

War of the Roses

While the roji* is meant to be a passageway
Altogether outside this earthly life
How is it that people only contrive
To sprinkle it with the dust of the mind.
　　　　　　　　　—Sen no Rikyu, sixteenth century

Briars arch to the ground and walk themselves, root by root, deep into the forest, where they bloom white stars across Sleeping Beauty's coffin. So it goes, for a hundred years. Then one day the prince breaks through the thorns and touches his lips to hers. Everything begins. Adam and Eve walk out of Eden, awake at last, prickly with their own power. And the bulldozers come, and Christiana Mall. And inside the mall, little oases of green, with fountains, standing for lost wilderness.

The mall and its sad, glittery lessons are only five miles from here. Still, whoever willingly turns back for long? We crave

---

*Literally, "dewy path." Poetic name for a tea garden.

civilization. We become fascinated with the workings of our brains, concocting what we hope is the ideal.

Nature's too crazy or too slow for us. Last year in the wake of Hurricane Floyd, two big trees fell across the creek behind our house. In ten years or so, grapevines and wild rose would have woven themselves through the branches; the trunks would have folded into the whole. We, of course, hired a tree service instead. This is what got me started.

I get an idea, I'm hell bent on it. Jerry's good-hearted and usually pitches in. We've been married for ten years, now. After turbulent past lives, we've come to value quiet. He makes coffee and sets out the breakfast things; I sew buttons back on his shirts, the order of our lives forever cast against the receding clank and chaos of our separate, private wars.

I begin to get an idea of how the stream area could look. Jerry begins to see it, too. Actually, ever since we bought the house four years ago, we've talked about opening up the space below us so that we can walk along the stream. We have two acres of woods. The house is built on the front of the land so that the wildness is all behind, down to the west branch of the Christina River—just a small stream here— and halfway up the hill on the other side. Since we moved in, we haven't once crossed the stream and walked across all of our land on the other side. The stream's just wide enough to make the leap across a little awkward, and there are the briars. In the winter when our grandsons are here, they want to explore. I've tried to show them the deer beds near the creek, but we come up against the stickers, and they want to turn back. You might say we're clearing for them.

Most of it's wild rose, anyway. *Rosa multiflora* was brought here from Japan, and Korea, and eastern China. During the thirties it was promoted as an inexpensive and dense "living fence" to contain livestock—*ikigaki*, the Japanese would have called it when they used it around their tea gardens. It was supposed to be good for sheltering pheasant, quail, and songbirds.

The trouble is, in this country it spreads like crazy, forming impenetrable thickets that drive out native plants. A lot of it got planted along roadsides for crash barriers, and now you can see it creeping inland, a great roiling white-flowered mass. Anywhere the land is disturbed, it moves in and takes over, sucking out soil nutrients, lowering crop yields in adjacent fields. The thorny stems stretch and arch downward, touching the ground and rooting, making bridges for themselves. For years, I admired the tapering clusters of flowers. I took pleasure in the sweet exaggerations of late spring, believing what I saw was a sign of health, of nature left alone for a change. "Look!" I'd exclaim. "Isn't that beautiful, all that wildness along the road."

Then I learned. It seems like a small piece of innocence to lose, but the stuff's growing everywhere, you begin to see that. You start seeing it as a sign of ruin. A few strands come up in the small mowed portion of our yard, then there's a bush. It's on the move. Down at the creek bank, it leans over, softening the line between earth and water, yearning for the other side, already dark and heavy with it. It blocks our way, its thorns hooking backward, holding our clothes, our skin, until we back up to release ourselves.

I call the agricultural extension. The man says, "You need to kill it. It'll choke out everything. Use Roundup." I worry about the stream. "Just don't spray it directly in the stream," he says. But I'm sure I do, sometimes. I pump up the container with air and get cocky with the wand, editing the landscape, eyeing everything with stickers and giving it a good dose. I fight my way to the backside of large clumps to spray from all angles. Where I can reach the water, I lean as far over as I can to get the webbed mass on the banks. I am on a death march across our property, with consequences I don't want to think about. But after a week or so, I watch the vines begin to sicken and die, and I love what I've done, how I've forced the world to behave itself. Still, I only make a dent. Most places, you still can't reach the creek.

What I have in mind is something like *Yarimizu*, an extremely old Japanese garden form usually appearing as a winding, narrow stream. A Japanese garden depends on the mindful placement of elements that, because of the confined boundaries, become a metaphor for the interplay of the interior world with the larger one.

I've noticed that a space looks smaller when it's wild, when there are no breaks for the eye, all brush and branches. Then you clear some of it out, establish an order, and it seems larger. Suddenly there's a something, with a nothing surrounding it.

> I placed a jar in Tennessee,
> And round it was, upon a hill.
> It made the slovenly wilderness
> Surround that hill.

Wallace Stevens knew that the eye enjoys its obstacles, that it believes in the demarcations as a sign of space. Also he knew that in no time, the obstacles take dominion.

Japanese gardens depend upon layering of experience. The five elemental phases of Chinese natural philosophy are earth, wood, fire, metal, and water: there's our post-and-beam cedar house; fire of sun on the windows, on their metal frames; and below the deck, the tease of water in the earth's crevice. The water, as in the pond at the entrance of some Zen temples, represents the threshold between the outside world and the inside realm of the sacred. I envision a stroll garden, a style developed in the Edo period. Walking through the garden results in a sequence of shifting scenes, which shouldn't be hard to replicate here. First, there are the chunky railroad-tie steps we had put in last summer that lead down to the path, then you walk almost horizontally, way off to the right through the trees down to the bridge. Having a bridge built was a necessary first step to getting beyond the low spot. It's like an expanse of dock, of good, sturdy treated lumber, a lot nicer than absolutely necessary, but solid. The bridge angles back left, crossing the skunk cabbage that shows up in the spring in the marshy area, the *numa*, in Japanese. Then come the thorns.

The previous owners had tried building a bridge across the actual creek, but the water rises and rushes too fast in a storm, and it was washed away. I'm trying to think of a more secure way to do it. A bridge across would give the sense of a Pure Land garden, also called a paradise garden, which is usually an island in a pond connected to shore by a bridge, signifying the possibility of salvation.

Indeed, I feel saved. Almost thirteen years ago, I moved out of the house I'd painted and patched and planted around— each room, each object, each small tree standing for some specific hope abandoned. I moved into a small apartment with my youngest child, my son, who was just starting college. After years of marriage, I was down to two twin beds, two dressers, one skillet, two saucepans, and half the books I was used to. I sat on the floor the day I moved in, sobbing. What was in my heart? A mixture of grief, terror, relief, and a faint bud of energy that felt like joy. It was the starting over, the chance to build civilization again out of chaos.

The world's raging with war: it's good to cut the perception down to the size of a tea garden. The details may possibly save us. Not the details themselves, but the quality of our attention to them. It may seem as if it's the details we're focusing on already, but the TVs are blaring, the cell phone's at our ear, we're hardly aware of anything in the blur. Who has time, or security of mind, to cut the attention down to one detail at a time, to let go of others, turn decisively to the object at hand, not filling it with our ideas, but letting it fill us with itself? What child wouldn't agree that the definition of love is attention? War, on the other hand, attends to nothing: it shuts down the immediate or we wouldn't be able to bear the suffering we inflict, or have inflicted upon us. We'd rebel and turn away, if we felt it fully. But no, we hover in the ideals—democracy, religion, our own sense of right. Let them take up the space, ideas floating, lazing along—sincere, certainly, possibly even right—but headed for smoke and vapor, more distance. The instruments of war, the tiny figures on their tiny tanks, become barely a blip on the horizon.

Meanwhile, in our peaceful life, when Jerry and I are both able to work at home, we go to our studies in separate corners of the house. At noon we meet for toast, oranges, and apples in the sunroom. As we face each other across the small maple table, I sometimes think of Gwendolyn Brooks's poem "The Bean Eaters"—the "old yellow pair" who "eat beans, mostly," and "keep putting on their clothes / And putting things away"—the quiet order people can come to, if they're lucky. In late winter, we look down at the dusting of snow, the "first flowers" as the Japanese would call them. What seemed once like distance appears to be only a few feet away, as if we could step off our high deck, float down like butterflies, and come to rest by the stream.

I call Stump-Be-Gone, up the road in Pennsylvania. Father and son show up. I take them on a tour, as far as we can get. "No way we can get a tractor, not even a small one, down here to clear this," they claim. "Hill's too steep." They give me the number of someone with a backhoe. So he comes out and looks. Prognosis the same, only subtler. "I'll call you with an estimate," he says, and never does. Even as we walk the land, I feel him drawing back, his "Well, I suppose we could . . ." and "I don't know. That's pretty steep for a backhoe . . . ," so I don't bother to call him back. The truth is, I don't call partly because a backhoe wasn't what I had in mind. I can imagine the wreckage.

I call the Stump-Be-Gone son back, who has a local number. Would you be willing to just bring your chain saw and cut up the fallen trees? I ask. He agrees to this, and I sweet-talk him after he gets here about going on down the way with the chain saw, just trimming back the vines. "It's so easy for you," I say, "and it would take us days and days with hedge trimmers." "Sure, well, I guess I could come back early, before I go to another job, as long as your neighbors don't mind hearing the saw at that hour," he agrees.

Dave's a tall, gentle-seeming man in his forties, with nice arm muscles and a pot belly. He wears a T-shirt with the sleeves ripped out, and sweats easily. His skin has that red, tense look of high blood pressure. You have the sense that in spite of his gentleness, the world has presented him with complexities he can't decipher, and that he's exploded, that he often explodes, and is sorry afterward. You get the sense there are lives left behind, for him. He drinks milk when he takes a break. I figure he has an ulcer. His words burst out as if he has to work at making them come. He has this job to do, and he'll do it, but I sense, as is often true when workmen are at the house, that I'm the one who most wants their friendship—well, at least their acknowledgement that we're both earning our keep. The laborers who are guests at our house are also our judges, silently sizing up the abstract things we appear to do with our hours. I attach myself to the computer with a special dedication while they are here, not to be thought useless. I try to think of things to say that unite us—the annoyance of the wild rose, for example. And the joy of seeing the creek.

He gets the trees cut up and partially stacked, leaving us a big pile of firewood. We carry what we can across the bridge and up to the back yard. But limbs and leaves still clog the creek. Jerry and I decide that before Dave comes back, we'd better finish that part of it, get that stuff out.

We put on duck boots, although they're immediately useless as we step into deep pools. We set up a system, throwing branches onto the far shore, where I stand, picking them up and throwing them further into the woods. The idea is to distribute them so that they don't seem to clump up anywhere. Another season and they'll be virtually gone. Jerry pulls branches out of the sludge on the bottom, tosses them to me. Pull and toss. I toss. I stomp down the pile. We have the water churned up, muddy. We fish around for imbedded branches under the muck. We pretend that it makes a difference to the stream, that the stream will appreciate being able to flow more directly, instead of meandering through the brush. The tiny fish swim somehow around us, invisible. It is a perfect day, warm and sunny, but not hot. We are bordered by wild rose. Jerry clips along the bank as we go, knowing that we'll have to let some of it grow back to prevent erosion.

Now he's pulling on a big branch, stuck in the water, held partly by the suction of mud. All at once, it gives way and slams back against his ribs. He doubles up with pain, trying to breathe. He climbs up the bank and sits in the sun, breathing, holding his side. Later, the bruise will begin, wide and purple.

Jerry's only four years older than I am, but things like this, I worry. Like every woman alive, I carry the statistics deep and silently in my heart—men's life expectancy compared to women's. And his parents died young, both of cancer. Add heredity to age: it's finally a matter of how long you're able to withstand the assaults of the world. I think about all those years Jerry smoked. It's what we carry with us that we can't get rid of. A late effect of tobacco. For the fish, it's the herbicides, the runoff from fertilizers, my Roundup. The more I learn the attention of love, the more I lurch out of control, helpless to prevent the pain of loss. Together, Jerry and I clear the path, the creek: we make it look as nearly as possible the way we want, briefly, on our way toward our own extinction.

On Thursday, Dave comes back. We hear him before we see him, revving up his saw. He thinks he can finish today. He starts off along the bank, whacking down wild rose. After a while, I get some coffee and walk down to see how he's progressing. He's brought his girlfriend this time, a plump blonde, about twenty-five, who sits on a stump, reading a fat novel with a colorful gilt cover. I offer her a Coke or coffee, but she pats the cooler. "We've brought everything we need," she says. I ask if she's bored, just sitting while he works. "No, he likes me to come along," she says, smiling. "I just read."

I'm at my computer, then, when he thuds up the stairs to the deck, red-faced and shirtless. "I ain't going back there," he blurts out. "Bees. Yellow-jackets, or something. They're all over. You'll have to get someone else to do it, because I ain't. Look," he says, pointing to the welts coming up on his arms and back. A dozen, maybe more. "Oh, oh, I'm so sorry," I say, "What can I do? What can I get you?"

Now he's calming down. "Oh, I have some stuff," he says. "I been stung before. But that's a mess of 'em you got there. In the ground. It's the buzz of the saw, it riles them up." I look around for his girlfriend. We walk back down, past the shirt he threw off, past the sunglasses he tossed in the path. She's still sitting with her book, Danielle Steele, I see. "If you just sit still, they'll ignore you," she says. And it seems to be true, although far down the path I see the stirring, and a few of them swarm in larger circles, almost reaching us.

"Okay, here's what you do," Dave tells me. "Pour a gallon or two of gas into a bucket. Come down here in the evening when they're quiet and pour the whole thing down the hole. That'll do it." He agrees to come back if I promise they're all gone. So after he leaves, as the sun goes down, I put on an old yellow rain-slicker snapped up to my chin, pull the hood over my head with a stocking cap underneath, and add long pants and gloves. I do this myself, even though Jerry volunteers. I got us into this, is my thinking. I pour gas in a bucket and walk carefully down to the path, to the end where the cutting abruptly stopped. All is quiet. One or two small wasps—they're wasps, not bees; I looked them up— meander in the air. I step gently to the hole, clearly visible in the leaves. I am helmeted, anonymous: a death machine for the second time, pouring gas down the hole, stepping back, then hurrying away. I'm at war, killing a whole colony of wasps. Part of my mind is numb with that knowledge, while the rest functions in simple, self-protective moves. I try not to exaggerate the significance, but my mind is full of dying wasps.

Dave comes back. I hear the whine of his saw before breakfast one day. When I go down, he's almost finished, a wide swath along the bank, debris everywhere alongside, severed grapevine trunks bleeding sap, the creek itself suddenly present, open, its melody audible. A frog hops into the water. One tree leans with its multiple trunks over the water, a large vine growing up its trunk and providing most of its foliage. Underneath, water rushes in a narrower funnel, singing, then widens and quiets. You can see it now, wider than I thought in places, our private piece of the stream meandering from Pennsylvania through western Newark and south into Maryland. Not that this is any distance. You can cross over into Maryland from the other side of our land, and Pennsylvania's just a half-mile up the road. Still, according to the law, this part is ours. You can't even walk through the middle of the creek without trespassing on our land, while the water continues on its way, owned and lost, owned and lost, over and over. The new head of the Department of the Interior once suggested that property owners have a "right to pollute." As if we could stop the results at our boundaries. As if boundaries were real.

We clear up to the very real fence. Our neighbors have strung barbed wire to the edge of the water and up the hill. They've padlocked the gate and nailed a No Trespassing sign on a tree. Their son, who was retarded, drowned in the creek years ago. We respect their right to be afraid, but the prettiest stretch of creek, with waterfalls and rapids, flows through their land. We walked there several times before we knew we shouldn't. Then they put the fence up. So we work within our small compass. Our mikiri, our trimming of bushes, frames the view.

Start at the beginning, now, down the twelve railroad-tie steps. You have to stoop slightly under the trees as you turn abruptly to the right, to the edge of our land. The path's covered with leaves. The ground's a thick cushion of loam. One concrete block balances your step onto the bridge. There is no reason for the indirect angle back to the left except to make it more interesting. On the other side of the bridge, the path now becomes firmer, particularly where we spread chips, and then you round the bend and there's the creek, coming out from under the willow and making a sharp curve where there's a little sludge of pollution and then curving sharply left and right again. It used to go mostly straight here and make a wider curve, before we cleared away the fallen trees. Now the water turns and rushes down a tiny waterfall of a buried log and spreads into two channels as it goes under the tree leaning across. Then the character changes again, to a wide glossy ribbon, where a frog jumps when you approach, and sometimes a snake slithers across to get out of your way. Here to the side is a hole big enough for a fox den; probably though, it's a groundhog hole, but it's so close to the water. The ground here is softer, more eroding, and we've placed logs to brace against further sliding. Up the other side is *nomine*, the peak of a low hill, beyond that, *no*, hillside fields, and a hawk, sailing. Beyond that is the subdivision of Glen Farms.

"I'll tell you what," I say to Jerry as we stand with our hands in our pockets on a cold day in November, watching minnows. "If we had a bridge across, a small deck over there, we could lie in the sun and watch the water. There's a lot more sun over there. I think we could anchor a bridge if we buried pilings in concrete on either side."

He pulls his cap back down over his ears. "Well, that's another year." He knows how to put me off until I burn out or find another project. But my mind keeps working. I hear the water trickling through the silence, neither kind nor unkind, neither interested nor uninterested, drawing me in, keeping me trying over and over to make something to frame its sublimity, its loneliness, its vast emptiness. I'm sure it's Pure Land over there.

There's a Japanese word, *aware*—the same as our word, but with a slightly different cast. It means an emotional response to the beauty of ephemeral things, the sadness that arises when you realize that nothing lasts. It's as inevitable as original sin. To be aware of beauty is simultaneously to love it and be nurtured by it, and to be cast out from it—to change it: paint it, take pictures of it, crop it, write it, edit it, make a garden of it—at the least, invest it with thoughts. Even at the subatomic level, as Heisenberg demonstrated, the act of observation changes the speed and/or the location of whatever is observed. He called this the Uncertainty Principle. The first glance at beauty changes it forever. To feel pleasure in beauty, to be really aware of it, is to be simultaneously sad.

Meanwhile, the deer keep coming. They seem to like the clearing. They're no fools—they can get to the water easier now, without the briars. They continue to bed down in the dried grapevines. We see their indentations, where they were just before we came.

Returning the Cats

I was the one elected to drive them to the Humane Association. We'd dreaded for days—as we always did—the prospect of getting them into their travel boxes. Over time, we'd devised a system that worked, albeit miserably for us all. We'd surreptitiously stash the boxes in the bedroom. I would station myself by the stairs to prevent either cat from running up to the loft or down to the basement. Jerry would go outside and ring the doorbell. At the sound of the tone, both cats would dash for the bedroom to hide under our bed—a king-sized bed with drawers underneath, leaving a two-foot passage in the middle between the drawers. We'd follow and shut the bedroom door, all of us inside. One of us would poke around under the bed with a broom, eventually driving a cat out at the head of the bed. The other would grab as the desperate cat emerged. Memphis was the most frantic. She'd leap with a tortured yowl to within a few feet of the ceiling, trying to climb the wall to get away. Between the two of us, we would finally get each one stuffed into his or her box.

I generally agree that cats read minds. On the way to the Humane Association, in utter terror, Toby pooped in his box. The sweet rotten-fruity smell began to waft forward in the car until I was sure what it was. Both cats were revved up into the agonized cry we've heard so many times before on the way to the vet's. But this, of course, went on longer, because this time I had to drive the twelve miles into Wilmington and wander around near the river to find the building again, a low, cement-block edifice on a rough street at the edge of town. When I got there, I knocked. No one answered. I set both forlorn boxes down on the pavement, knocked louder. Finally, a young woman appeared. "I know they normally don't do intakes until 11:00, but I was told I could come early to leave the cats," I told her. "Someone was to have left a note about it." She looked for the note, couldn't find it. Reluctantly, she let me in. I went back out to the car to get Memphis's blanket, the brown Polartec one she always slept on in the big living room chair. The door locked behind me. While I was pounding on it again, the intake person drove up. Again I explained.

"I'm sorry," she said. "We can't take any pets today. We've had a leak in the ceiling and have to move all the animals." I was now a fifty-nine-year-old woman about to sob like a baby. "I can't take them back," I gasped out. Of course I could have, but it was so hard to get to this point, I couldn't imagine doing it again. I figured she thought there was some terrible domestic problem that getting rid of the cats was solving, or causing. She sighed, began filling out the papers for readmission. Actually, she had to take the cats—although maybe not this very day—because when we adopted them, we were asked to sign an agreement to return them to the Humane Association if we couldn't keep them.

Someone came for the boxes. At the last minute, I remembered to call out, "They like each other. Put them together." How terrible if I'd forgotten. They'd never lived a day without each other. "How long ago did you adopt the cats?" the woman asked, working on the forms. "Six years," I replied.

Six years ago, my husband's daughter Amy was visiting from Pullman, Washington. Amy the cat lover determined that we'd been too long without furry things in our house and headed us to the Humane Association to enrich our lives. We'd both had pets many times. Jerry had had a farm, even, for ten years, with cows and rabbits. This was before our separate divorces. Jerry had left behind, besides his wife, an aged, beloved dog. Not long after, his former wife and children had had to have her euthanized. The "funeral" was held without Jerry, one of the small punishments no one labels as such, but still. I'd left behind two cats, one of them "mine," because the apartment I found didn't allow pets. My former husband reported that Giselle was pooping in the corners and on the bed and was probably going to go crazy. We were all crazy—I couldn't spend much time feeling miserable about the poor cat. I'd loved her dearly, dearly enough, I'd hoped, to make up for my husband's intense favoritism toward his cat, Connie, named for Constance Chatterley in D. H. Lawrence's novel.

Since then, my new husband Jerry and I had cat-sat for my sister and her husband's expensive blue tabby for almost a year while they were in Scotland. Lewis became Jerry's shadow during his sabbatical year, while he was home writing a book. Creatures love Jerry. He was convinced he had a pet toad who would wait for him outside the sliding doors to his study.

Cats are the easiest of pets, generally. With Amy's help, Jerry and I picked out two gray tabbies from the Humane Association, brother and sister, about four months old—cats found outside and rescued, we were told. They'd been in a cage almost since birth, but they both responded when we picked them up. The male was big-boned, with coarse fur. The female, clearly the runt, was skinny and more shy, but still responsive. We named them Tobias, for Tobias Smollett, the British novelist my husband specialized in—a far cry from Lawrence—and Memphis, a nod to Elvis. I had just finished a book of poems about Elvis.

I have to say, we're both good to animals. We live a quiet life. We're gentle. We bought those fishing-pole cat toys with feathers on the end and had both kittens leaping several feet in the air and chasing madly around the house as we dragged the feathers like wounded birds. Neither cat

would come to us, but we figured patience would pay off.
Eventually, they quit hiding from us, although they continued to run for cover when a strange car drove up, or the
doorbell chimed.

We have a sunroom we close off at night, to save heat. Toby
and Memphis would make a point of being in that room at
bedtime. It required strategic planning to get them out.
Sometimes we would drag the feather toy, hoping they'd
chase it out of the room. If that didn't work, we'd pretend to
go to bed, leaving the door to the sunroom open just a crack.
After a few minutes, sometimes half an hour, they would
decide to wander through, and we could close up. Sometimes we'd call them for treats in the kitchen. Sometimes it
would work. Different nights, different strategies.

For almost four years, before we had them declawed,
we regularly clipped their claws. Several days before, we'd
start planning. On the afternoon of the clipping, we'd sit
in our chairs, pretending nothing was up, talking quietly
to each other. I, being the quickest, would get up and meander toward whichever cat, usually Toby, so let's say Toby,
was the most settled. If I was lucky, I'd catch him. But this
is what I mean, that cats can read minds. Often, he'd perk
up his ears and run off. We'd have to wait. If I dove for him
and missed, we'd have to wait days more. Jerry would put
on gloves. He would hold Toby as firmly as possible on the
small table in the sunroom. I would clip. Often, we emerged
scratched and bloody. Sometimes, in the wild squirming,

I'd miss and cut too deeply into the nail, drawing blood. I'd feel terrible about it. Toby would leave little pads of blood across the floor. Memphis would run and hide as soon as she heard Toby cry out from being caught. We would have to wait several hours to try with her. We hated to grab her by using treats for bait, but sometimes we would.

Memphis adopted me, and Toby adopted Jerry. Memphis would dodge away if I reached for her, and would very rarely climb in my lap, but if I sat at my computer, she figured I was safely occupied and would jump in my lap, rub against my hands, and drool on my keyboard. I didn't have the heart to push her away. I often typed with the additional small weight of a cat's head draped across my hand. Toby, on the other hand, would consent to being petted only through bars—reminiscent, I suppose, of the bars of the cage he lived in the first few months of his life. He would perch himself on our stairs and happily let us stroke his back as long as we reached safely through the rungs. He would lie on a rocking chair and let us pet him by reaching from behind through the bars on the back. He would finally even turn on his stomach to be rubbed.

The first year we had the cats, Jerry had a normal teaching load, which meant he was home a fair amount. Then he became chair of the English department and was gone all day most days. Toby began peeing in his study, saturating the oriental rug. If we had overnight guests, either cat might pee or poop on any one of the rugs. Should we give them daily tranquilizers? We'd never catch them. And since they would eat only dry food, how could we mix drugs in? We tried plug-in pheromone diffusers in two part of the house, at twenty-five dollars each, changed once a month. They didn't seem to make any difference. The house began to smell, not like pheromones.

Oppression creeps into such situations. It would be no different if they had been troubled teenage children or senile parents. The oppression is a mixture of guilt and anger. Maybe we should play with them more. Maybe we should call the vet again. We felt helpless and rejected. I cleaned up the third pile on the oriental rug, blotting carefully so as not to smear the wool dyes. I sprayed with enzyme odor remover, knowing the smell would never completely go away. I was angry. I'd done my best. The cats looked at me with blankly transparent eyes. Whenever I stepped across the floor a little too quickly, they frantically darted away as if I were a monster, even after all my gentle rubbing and sweet-talking, They ducked when I reach down to pet them. How dare they? Okay, they were feral. Can trust never be earned? Daily, we were confronted with the absolute, irreconcilable Other.

Years ago, my uncle and aunt adopted a little girl, an act of charity, really, since they had two of their own already. They discovered after a long string of difficulties that the child had fetal alcohol syndrome. As she grew, she lied, stole, and finally ran away with any number of men. They stuck by her the best they could, even sending her money as an adult when she got in scrapes. They'd made a commitment and weren't about to forget it. Likewise, the Humane Association chose the word adoption to imply a serious commitment. As with a marriage, we're intended to make it lifelong. Giving it up is a process. We do it by degrees, almost invisibly at first. Up to the day I left my marriages—both of them—part of me believed I could somehow make things work. I ebbed and flowed, from peace (We're going to be fine; I do love him) to misery (This can't go on; I'll die), spiraling downward. Part of me began to know it was hopeless, but knew not to speak it to myself, because I would have to act before my spirit was ready. One day a door shut in me, and I couldn't go back through. I hardened my heart and left. It felt one-sided—I was doing the leaving—but truly it wasn't.

A commitment to an animal is indeed one-sided. Humans, not animals, are the ones who make choices to accept or reject. Generally, an animal that's fed and petted won't leave. That's not choice, that's instinct. Contrary to the sentimentalists' point of view, a human's choice to accept or reject a pet is pretty much based on reason—"I want this cute thing in my lap, I want a companion, I want to feel needed, I want to be greeted at the door when I come home," and so on. But once that choice is made—like an arranged marriage—we do fall in love. Usually we do. We're willing to make sacrifices for our pets. Jerry and I did love our cats. We called to them as soon as we walked in from school. We baby-talked to them. We petted them for as many minutes as they were willing to give it a try. We gave them treats before bed. Daily, we cleaned their litter boxes (one each, to try to cure the "accident" problem). We took them to the vet. Didn't we love them? Certainly we took care of them, did the best we could for them, the way we did for our children when they were still at home. Who can say where the line is between love and a deep, ingrained habit of responsibility?

Yet we gave them back, after all those years. We don't know what's happened to them. Neither of us wants to find out. When we adopted the cats, they showed us a room for the ones deemed—maybe after trial and error—"unadoptable"—a large carpeted space with boxes stacked up and things to climb on. There were probably twenty-five cats there when we looked: sleeping, meandering around. What about the others? So many unwanted cats. What about the people we once wanted, yet left behind? Who can ever say we did the right or the wrong thing, to give up when we did? All the thinking and arguing with oneself goes on long before the act. When one finally makes a move, the movement is all.

The day I left my second marriage, I lay rigid for hours on the chaise lounge in the sunshine. What I was thinking was anyone's guess. This is probably what happens before a soldier goes to war—a deep concentration begins, a focus so primal that it has neither words nor motions. When my husband slid the patio door open and came out, we smiled at each other, the wan smile of the doomed. He knew what I would say. This is what fear looks like after the bristling, screeching, and scratching are done. It plunges inward, it draws itself down to a point so lonely it accepts only itself for company. If it is the good kind of fear, it's full of action— slow-motion, deliberate, seemingly robotic. It's the body taking over, for a while, to make sure the mind is okay.

I once had a cat named Sneakers. She was forever having kittens because my father refused to spend money on spaying. Hard to believe, but true. When Sneakers had kittens, my father would put them in a large cooking pot with a rag soaked in formaldehyde until they quit squirming. Then he would bury them. I say this as if he did it regularly. I can't remember. He did it once, at least, when I was twelve. I remember my body taking over, running as fast as I could for blocks and blocks, while he was doing it. But there was no escape from the small mound of dirt in the back yard when I returned. I have never determined whether my father is completely a monster or not. Sometimes he is, sometimes he isn't. When I was maybe thirteen, Sneakers had a litter of kittens, one of which I loved dearly and wanted to keep. "Keep whichever you want, but we can only have one," my father said. I chose the kitten, all tiny and fluffy. My father took his rifle. I heard a blast, heard a scuffle as Sneakers, wounded, ran under the house, my father on his hands and knees after her. Another blast. Sitting on my bed holding the kitten, I was thinking nothing at all. Whatever I was feeling had no place to go. I had made a choice. I was stuck with my father, my guilt, my kitten, my grief. I rubbed the kitten's fur against my cheek.

If my father could kill kittens, could kill Sneakers, what is his commitment to his children? How different are children from cats? Where's the line? If I could make this choice to save one kitten and kill the mother we'd already committed ourselves to, what are the depths of disloyalty inside me? Of badness?

I know how badness works. It's accomplished by a closing of the mind, little by little, a turning away. The larger and harder question is "What does bad mean?" When, for example, is it okay to leave a marriage? When, for example, does it become not okay to abort a child? The Catholic church used to say that spilling your seed on the ground is a sin—even the possibility of a child is sacred. It still says that stopping an egg and a sperm from uniting is a sin. Is it a sin to use the "morning after" pill? Is it sinful to abort a fetus? Is sinful to abort at two months? Three months? Is it sinful to gently put a pillow over a hideously deformed newborn's head? And when, for example, is it okay to go to war? These questions are all about commitment. To ourselves, to each other, to life. When and where does our commitment begin and end?

I think of Memphis and Toby daily. They're shadows in the corner, a rustle of papers. The Humane Association has become for me a silent room in my mind, full of sorrow. I think the move may kill them, at least one of them. We abandoned a commitment. There were waverings and circlings in our decision. We almost decided several times. Gradually, over the last few years, the number of our grandchildren grew to ten. We began to feel overwhelmed with responsibilities. When do we get to have free space for ourselves, with nothing to look after? I can't deny that this helped determine our decision—and the fact that we'd decided to spend much more time in Michigan at our cottage where we couldn't take indoor cats. Finally, as people do, we came upon a final trigger—our son-in-law was found to be seriously allergic to cats and couldn't come in our house without suffering.

In any case, I'm not sorry. We made the choice, the way people of general good will always make choices, by weighing alternatives. We assumed that the quality of our lives is more important than the quality of our cats' lives. This isn't fair. Taken to the farthest limit, the destruction of animal life on our planet is based on the same premise, and such thinking will kill us all, finally. The other extreme, I guess, is unfettered and unmolested cows wandering the streets of India, hundreds of deer munching on forsythia in the suburbs. Should we eat meat? Should we eat any living thing? Taken to the wildest extreme, do we deserve to live when so many are dying?

Every day that I see fly-covered children on TV starving, I feel guilty. Every time I think of my past errors in judgment, I feel guilty. A cat can make you feel guilty for living. It can eye you as if you haven't quite met its expectations. It can open one eye, that is, and close it again as if its interior world is far preferable. You never know. So you project upon them what you will, demons or spirits. The demons or spirits rub your leg, a little tease, and dart away. Actually, this is pretty much the spot we're in as humans, anyway. We wander alone on this planet with our massive, reflective brains. We make choices, day by day, on the best evidence we have. Our little choices—sometimes only nuances of attitude delicate as the flap of a butterfly's wing—lead to big shifts, that lead ultimately to life or death. We simply make them, and hope that we haven't hindered the universe much in its yearning toward the good.

Showgirls

The last showgirls in Vegas, the ones that just dance, are about done for. There's only one show that still uses them. They're like a museum act, quaintly depending only on the movements of their own bodies, plumes and tassels notwithstanding. If you want something in Vegas these days, you invent it out of more electrified and electrifying parts than the human body can offer. Invention is the desert's trick: there's nothing but sand here, inviting mirage and magic. Even from the early days, if you wanted girls, you went to the whorehouses only a block off the strip, the ones still advertised in flyers handed out at every corner. You made the girls into whatever you wished. Today, if you want a show, you raise your eyes to the huge neon signs, rolling and flashing, first one thing, then another, Neil Diamond, then Cirque du Soleil, in blue, green, red-orange, suspended and turning from cables.

Inside the Venetian, you sit at a café on a canal where gondolas pass by poled along by singing gondoliers. Above, a perfect sky so high and real you have to spot the buttons to see that it's fastened there, a vast tent of sky. If you wanted birds, too, someone could probably make them for you. Outside the Wynn, a fake mountain rises from the pavement, flush with real trees and a high waterfall dashing over fake rocks, like a 3-D I-Max, more weirdly real than the real thing. The falls feed into a stream that enters the complex and winds along to an indoor lake. Inside, there's a huge, plummeting sheet of water, a wall of water. Four naked human sculptures stand in the wide pool at its base, each deeper in than the next, facing the sheet of water as if it were the latest idea of God: blank and silent, what you finally face. Unless you get there at certain hours of the evening, when snippets of Swan Lake and other classics play, along with a light show. Or you can stop in at the Catholic Church nearby, as I do, partly because it's cool in there. The windows are all shards of color, the figures muscular, square-jawed, faintly Latino, another direction for the mind to go in its dizzying elaborations.

My sister is dizzy again. She calls me in tears. She hates to be so down on my birthday, when I'm away, alone, but her eyes are jumping around and she has no energy. Her blood pressure is too low. It's the hormones messed up again. The surgery to remove a brain tumor and the stroke following almost completely destroyed her pituitary, causing her body to lurch from one near-disaster to the next. She's gaining weight from the Prednisone. She looks at her once-beautiful body and tries to accept. She takes the pills, does what she's told, but still, *her* body has become *the* body, a product of doctors, pills, and machines.

On the wall by one entrance to my hotel, there's a chorus line of "Crazy Girls" in bronze with the bronze caption, "No if, ands, or . . ." The women are turned away from us, the front halves of their bodies pressed into the wall, their exposed rear ends bare and perfect. It's all about wishes, what a person would want for a birthday present, I guess. In the desert, there's nothing to disguise naked wishes. When the whole world is made out of nothing, it wishes hard to be something.

The old ladies with walkers, old men in wheelchairs, the ones with oxygen tanks, are smoking and drinking and playing the jazzed-up multicolored slot machines, desire all over their faces like jam, a little money rolling their way, a river of possibilities. Nothing lasts anyway, it's all hotels along here, and nobody stays for too many nights.

My sister's life remains precarious. When she came home from the hospital, she used a wheelchair, then a walker. The first time she made it up the stairs alone, her husband cried. She uses a cane now. The room lurches if she turns her head too quickly. She has an inner ear condition (caused by the disruption of the surgery) that can be helped by certain exercises, but they don't completely fix it. Every day she makes a list of the day's activities. After decades as

a high school English teacher, she's adrift, trying to create her own meaning. Her book about teaching methods
just came out last winter, but she can't go to conferences
to talk about it, and she can't accept invitations to lecture.
She gets too tired. Her eyes jump. She's had to retire from
teaching. What now? She does her eye exercises, lifts her
small weights. She does her stretches, works her crossword
puzzles to aid her cognitive recovery. She writes thank-you
notes, printing because her handwriting has never quite
recovered. She walks to the grocery store to bring home a
backpack full of groceries. She folds clothes. She has begun going to church. She meditates.

Once, sitting on the porch of a cottage on Lake Winnipe-
saukee, a friend said to me, "I get up every day figuring out
who I am, what I will be." This is what my friend and I had
in common, a childhood that left us uncertain, that had us
making ourselves up out of nothing.

That's what my sisters and I have in common. If we ask our
father to tell any anecdote about our childhood, he can't.
He can't remember how old we are. He doesn't remember
birthdays. This is not because of his age: he's never done
these things. All three of his daughters grew up waving feel-
ers in every direction, throwing ourselves this way and that,
trying to figure out who we were, what we should be. I threw
myself upon the sea of sex, thinking it was love. I threw myself into the boat of matrimony, thinking it would keep me

from sinking. I was a showgirl: look at me, you can have me. Look at me, I'm a model of a married woman, young but responsible, I can sew, I can bake, I can cut my own hair. I go to church, even.

Yesterday it was 117 degrees on the Strip. I decide to take a long exercise walk today at six in the morning, but even so, it is almost a hundred. This early, drunks are still curled, asleep, in the concrete corners. I notice how still they seem, peaceful, actually, like dead people, no snoring or twitching. The street cleaner has not yet swept up last night's bottles, cans, and flyers. The air has a sticky-beer flavor. The sky is a pinkish haze, as if the sun hasn't so much risen as swollen back into yesterday's casing. Four concrete mixers are lined up behind an suv at a red light. When the light turns, the suv sits there. Honking begins. Honking goes on. At last, a driver gets out and walks forward to the suv. The driver, a woman, is slumped over the wheel, asleep. She jerks herself awake and drives off. I worry about the world, this one small manifestation.

I haven't yet said what I'm doing here in Vegas on my birthday. I give lectures on poetry for the International Society of Poets. I wrote an exposé of this same organization back when I was in grad school, for the local underground newspaper. For the basis of my story, I'd sent the International Library of Poetry (same group) a poem: "Oh my darling sweetie, / you have such smelly feeties, / Please put on your socks / or you'll stop all the clocks." It was accepted for their anthology. If I wanted to see my poem in print, I'd have to buy the book at a price of forty dollars.

I was recruited to lecture at ISP by a poet I respect, who told me there were going to be changes, and that we could all help. The organization wanted a few poets with PhDs and long résumés, to lend legitimacy to their extravaganza conferences. But Lord, the first time I went, in Washington DC, I walked in to a poetry Vegas, everyone clamoring to read, to win prizes, no one wanting to listen, people in their spangled poet clothes, wearing large beribboned name tags that said "Poet." The ones who'd already read their poems before judges carried around their grotesquely huge trophies. Each person got one. At the banquet, Florence Henderson inducted new members into the Society, while everyone waved Day-Glo wands in the air to represent "the light of poetry." A magician performed, the Drifters sang. I came home telling wry stories, but also strangely moved. As I'd talked with participants, I sensed a deep desire commingled with the egomania. They really wanted to learn how to write good poems. They wanted to be shown some good poems.

I give lectures on meter and rhyme, on how to make a story work as a poem, on the beginning craft of writing poems. My most popular lecture is on getting published. Everyone wants to be published. Desperately. All writers do. But the hunger isn't really for that, as we know if we stay at this long enough. That's the stage show. When the lights go down and we go home, we want to know we've done well, that we've learned something about doing well. We want to make this meaning for our lives. We want the world to tell us we've done well, of course. How else do we measure? But we need to know it for ourselves.

I watch the women here at the slots, particularly them. Particularly the ones in wheelchairs, the ones with walkers. Who am I, I think, to walk through the casino arrogant as Dante through the deepening terraces of hell? Who was I to tell wry stories about the "poets" at ISP? It is actually love, isn't it, whatever we picture at the pinnacle of what we desire: the pearly gates, the mile-high stack of chips, the Pulitzer Prize. Underneath is an underground river, the prizes not won, the candles not lit, the touch denied, oh, if only.

If only my sister had emerged from the surgery with more of her pituitary left. If only her brain hadn't seized that night as it coped with the trauma of surgery, hadn't triggered a stroke. The smallest waver of difference can change a life forever. Where the wheel stops, which card is dealt.

The prize for the winning poem at the ISP convention is twenty thousand dollars. Those of us who judge read more than three hundred of the finalist poems, the ones chosen by other judges at the small-session readings. We do this in the late afternoons, on into dinnertime, reading, making notes, assigning numbers. Some poems we give the lowest score of 1 to instantly: the Hallmark ones, the ones that can't even get a cliché right, that can't keep the meter they start with, the ones with multiple fonts, flowers down the side of the page and gross misspellings or misuse of words. The poems that fall into the 2–3 range are the ones that have an idea, not original, usually, but at least carried through with some control of the language. For the top five prizes (all big money) we're looking for—what?—we eat our sandwiches, drink Diet Cokes, and go on for hours, trying to decide. We read poems aloud to each other to find a few that might fall into the 5 range.

Billy Collins, in his discussion of how he chose poems for *The Best American Poetry, 2006*, says he was looking for a human voice, a sense of manifest content, a degree of surface clarity. He wants poems that don't sound like "a Swedish movie run backwards with no subtitles," but also he doesn't want to be bored by poems that are transparent from beginning to end. All five of us judges would agree. But the question—What are we looking for?—is more basic than that. As Collins went on to note, we have more trouble with the word "poetry" than with the word "best." We're dealing with a lot of Robert Service look-alikes here. A few of them are good at it.

The Robert Service poems locate us in a world that has ceased to exist, may never have existed. They feel as out of place as Smokey the Bear in Vegas. Yet there's something attractive in their simple narratives. Tony Hoagland explains it this way: "It is precisely my own private, internalized 'postmodernity'—my short attention span, my rootless life, my neural disarray, my ruins and fragments—that have led me, increasingly, to value the material world in poems." When he was younger, he says, having no distance from the real, he wanted to escape or deface it. Now he craves information and arrangement. He loves poems that "locate, coordinate, and subordinate." I know what he means. Service could fall into that category, too.

No matter how the poem tries to do it, we keep hoping for the ones that deeply locate and explore the Truth that is Beauty, the Beauty that is Truth. God help us. It's hard enough to judge whether the surface glitter—if there is any—only floats and scatters, or whether it traces some outline of real bone.

Millie tries to quit crying. She always asks about what I'm doing. I tell her we're down to the last of the judging, that we have only a small stack for this evening to get through. She asks if I like any of the poems. Yes, I tell her, there are a few that give me some real pleasure. What is it about those, she asks? They have a strong voice, I say, some of the metered ones do it well, and best of all, a few of them sometimes surprise me.

Here I am, several light years out in space. Against the struggle for survival, I offer only aesthetics. Against a sea of slot machines, I offer lectures on poetic form. Against my sister's loss and pain, I offer, what, a few minutes' distraction? Pleasure is something Millie has had little of, for a long time. When she first came home from the hospital, she thought that if she faithfully did her exercises, she would gradually get to be almost as good as new. A year later, we know that's not the case. She can never even drink a glass of wine again, can never again go out in her and her husband's sailboat, maybe never drive.

Is there any adequate palliative for a hard life? I sit at the bar later and have a glass of wine, my birthday present to myself, keeping my eye on one woman at her slot machine. She's set up for the long haul, cigarette and drink beside her, coins stacked. She must be about seventy, white hair raggedly reaching her shoulders, thin legs in thin white jeans, feet in red backless scuffs, toenails matching the shoes. She doesn't look up or away all the time I watch her. She stays focused on the machine, its rolling images. I can't see the images from here, and only part of her deeply lined face, illuminated by the flashing lights. Her eyes are very light blue, I think. They seem transparent, as if she's soaked up by the lights. I don't know if she's happy. I don't know if she has a hard life. I don't know if she's addicted to this or if she's out for a lark. I can project anything I wish upon her.

I wonder about her idea of beauty. If this room is beautiful to her, if the Strip is beautiful to her. I wonder if there are

more versions of happiness than are dreamt of in my philosophy. I imagine this woman telling me yes, she's happy,
and yes, playing the slots is all the meaning she needs. She
likes it. She might win. It's exciting. Beautiful. Palliative?
She's never heard the word.

As I'm walking down the Strip—not my early walk, but later—
a drunk college-age student wants to high-five me. Okay. A
couple of Asian tourists ask me to take their picture. Okay.
Couples with peculiar hair and tattoos pass me, entwined
and giggling. Sometimes I think the world is a birthday party,
a silly one with hats and M&Ms, one I've refused the invita-
tion to because I'd feel awkward there. I act like a nun in the
middle of a world made expressly for my pleasure.

I am acting like one now. I am not in Vegas, of course. That's
past. I'm remembering. I'm sitting at my computer in the
bedroom of the cottage, where I can't see the lake. This
is so I can get some work done. Yet it's out there, beauti-
fully serene this morning, the sun bright and eager over the
pine trees. That, and people are lined up at slot machines,
and people are building huts on tropical islands with TV
cameras recording their survival, and people are carrying
around huge trophies that attest to the winning nature of
their poem. People are getting drunk.

   I have gotten drunk occasionally. I would like to get drunk
for my sister. To leave this earth for an invented one with
softer edges, a more malleable kind of Truth. I would like

to write a poem that does that. The foul rag and bone shop of the heart? Note that Yeats didn't go there. He went to the poem, he invented the poem to talk *about* the rag and bone shop. The poem is a circus of glitter and subterfuge. It dances off the ends of the earth carrying its heavy load. But it doesn't fall, because it imagines rising.

Private Bath

For example, when we were at that chic old B&B in Kensington, I had to wrap my slippery, thin traveling robe around me and head down the hall past the half-dozen other rooms, hoping to God no one was in the bathroom during my morning window of personal opportunity. If we happened not to leave the area during the day, I'd come back and try again, ears tuned before I got all the way up to the landing for the ominous sound of water running. Whether we were in Kensington Palace or at a coffee shop on the corner, I would remain alert for an obscure bathroom, one on a lower level, with poor lighting, one that could be easily overlooked, that I might have to myself. I grew up in a family of six with one bathroom. I always, still, sincerely wish to beat everyone out, and to have them go away. Conscience troubles, but doesn't deter me.

At the lake, too, it's always been pretty much the same. I dearly love the outhouse, with its high window so that the other world is nothing but the tops of trees. I love the rich

smell of accumulation, mixed with earth, everything changing back into itself. But if someone knocks at the outhouse
door, even if they politely drift down the hill pretending not
to wait, I'm trapped by time. No longer is time open-ended,
no longer are all things possible, but now are expected. I
have an assignment—to finish my business, to be a member of the give-and-take of human society.

Imagine, Grandfather built the outhouse with three holes
and a dial on the outside of the door that points to—or used
to before the letters faded—Women or Men, as if several
would like to use it at the same time!

This is not a problem of my body. Out there is the *out there*:
the angry and crying parents, the prostitution rings, the
former husbands. In here is *in here*. Thomas Merton said
that as soon as you're alone, you're with God. Something
there is that does like a wall, that resolutely stacks up the
stones. I acknowledge the evils: the old-stone-savage ran-
cor of patriotism, the slamming door of privilege, the im-
perious altar screens of religion. But at home in my own
bathroom, I'm Rodin's Thinker under the glorious sun of
the heat lamp, bending over Doonesbury, Dilbert, Boon-
docks, the glassy ease of *Metropolitan Home*, the Tao Te
Ching, with its speechless Chinese calligraphy edging the
pages like lace—the world at last manageable size, sparsely
furnished with chrome toilet holder, carefully folded green
towels, butcher-block countertop. I balance on the edge of

the seat, between feeling and action, between intimacy and the revelation of nature.

When my friend Joan went to Russia several years ago, she reported that in the public bathrooms, people squatted over open holes in the floor. All over the world people crouch in gullies, in plain view, nothing to wipe with. Understand, I'm not shy with my body. I'm not shy about letting my bare breasts flop around in the locker room at the gym. I can walk and talk as if *out there* were my world. As if the world behind the bathroom door is only a product of a mind embarrassingly helpless to control the very creation that supports it. I don't need quiet out there, I need quiet in my soul. I need time and space, the brief illusion of eternity. To sit on the cliff of the toilet, disenchantment only a door away. No one wants eternity for an eternity. Just to feel it, to touch its walls with some regularity is enough. Also, lots of times when I am at a party, I stand with my wine glass among the quite interesting people and their interesting stories, and my soul sits down inside the small cloister of my body, watching the door.

Where You Are

To know where you are (and whether or not that is where you should be), is at least as important as to know what you are doing.
—Wendell Berry

Part of me definitely doesn't want to begin again, about my father. He's eighty-nine. Enough said, you'd think, if you'd read all I've written about him already. Let him sit at his dining room table typing single-spaced screeds disproving Einstein and God, and ranting about the awful Bush administration. Let him take notes on the cardboard dividers from Shredded Wheat boxes. Let him watch the news in peace on his twenty-year-old fourteen-inch TV. Let him read *National Geographic* and *Wooden Boat* magazines, drop them on the floor, and leave them there forever.

He drives three days a week for Meals on Wheels and eats lunch at the Senior Center, where his job is to post the menu every day. I'm sure many of the old folks know who he is, an emeritus professor from the local university. The seniors must find him kind and gentle, often funny, and weirdly interesting, but not the kind of person you can figure how to get close to.

I drive from Michigan to Missouri, twelve hours, to see him. I figure I can make some small headway on cleaning out his junk. I work on it all day Friday, carrying things out, piling them in the dumpster I've rented. Saturday morning, he greets me at the bottom of the stairs: "You might as well just take me out and throw me on the heap right now. You've gotten rid of everything that matters to me." Ach! A natural mistake, as I plowed downward through the Dantean circles of his basement. How to calculate where limbo ends and utter damnation begins? On top, the layer as tall as I am, are limp and bent cardboard boxes stuffed with filthy rags, chenille bedspreads, unused paper cups and plates; an old mixer; a meat grinder; empty glass bottles; glass bottles filled with what used to be plum preserves; two rotten canvas tents; various boards of various sizes; a large model sailboat, sails rotted; a homemade ladder used the last time he single-handedly reroofed the house; an ancient bike, a bike wheel. The upper reaches, disturbed, shift and collapse.

Upstairs, there are two shoe boxes in his "junk room," one overflowing with tire weights, one with combs. He's picked them up in the streets. Why throw away perfectly good tire weights, good combs? He washes the combs. The tire weights he uses to balance his own tires. He's rigged up an old-fashioned glass Coke bottle with a tiny round piece of plywood on top with a spike in it. He has another round piece of plywood he centers the wheel on, and sets it on the spike, on the Coke bottle. As the wheel tips, he corrects the tipping with the weights. It works better than the machines at the garage, he says. The leftover weights pile up in their box like fierce eyebrows. You can dip into the combs and feel them slide around like shale: black, white, red, green, clear.

I will never get this right. He'll slip away again. I'll be as exact as his example taught me to be: I'll list the objects, touch their hard edges with the edges of my words. They'll nudge each other, winking at what's unsaid between them. They know this is about me, still trying to find a parent, some point of origin under the rubble.

I thought the "good" tools were in the garage side. I should have realized that the drill with a broken, exposed electrical cord was the "good" one. And the dozen or so dulled, paint-covered screwdrivers and pliers. I cart them back from the dumpster. My sister Michelle arrives from Texas. We descend again, wearing dust masks and gloves. We take out eight backbreakingly heavy bundles of shingles. We fill two trash cans with clear glass, another with plastic. We put this out for recycling. The glass container falls over and rolls down the steep hill. I pick up the shards.

We reach the floor's caked, dried mud. The walls are full of cracks that pour water when it rains, creating a swamplike river Styx. My father has drilled holes into the basement walls and stretched heavy wire, using turnbuckles, across the worst of them; he has smeared the area with epoxy in an attempt to slow down the widening. My heretic sister and I have no faith. The basement is sliding down the hill.

Our father has no faith either. "Malthus was right. Too many people in the world," he says, to start with. Then there are the idiots waging wars, the ignorant economic policies, the depletion of the oil supply, and so on. We are in the ninth circle. My father has placed wooden platforms to keep things off the floor. Under these are the remains of walnuts, once in a bag in one corner, carried by animals, maybe, all over, and rotted to a pervasive black powder. I use a snow shovel to scrape up the mixture of mud and sootlike powder.

When I was a child, I would take advantage of the few times he and my mother were both out of the house to clean as best I could. But what was important, what not? All I could do was stack up papers, dust around oilcans and armatures, vacuum the space not filled with boxes and magazines. I was Joan of Arc, this my exhausting personal crusade.

I'm already tired. It's barely two months since my husband Jerry and I cleaned out our own lives, retiring from our long careers as university professors and moving halfway across the country, from Delaware to northern Michigan. We are in this limbo for now: no career, no history. We gave half our furniture to our children, bought a smaller house. We now live an hour from the old family cottage, the one Michelle and I cleaned out a few years ago, trailer-load by trailer-load, the same way. I've spent the last few years digging out, beginning again.

It's not really a beginning, in Michigan, with the history of the cottage behind me, all the years of summers—I've come back. Can a person return? To return to the past is to lose it. To clean out and fix up the old cottage was to sacrifice the sacrosanct status of memory. To put the past into words is to lose everything that doesn't fit.

We sweep my father's basement, a fog of dust. There is grief in me, like a fog. Where can it be found, exactly, the grief of letting go of my career, the town and friends I've had for over thirty years? The simple grief of living this life, the grief of my father's life, its accumulations? Is it in my muscles, my lungs, the constriction around my heart? I study it the way I study the aches coming on with age.

Especially if your parents are a fog to you, you hold onto place even more tightly. In 1978, my volatile and quickly acquired new husband, my children, and I made the long trip from Arkansas to Delaware. I'm feeling again now the numb pain of it, of leaving the town that had anchored me since I was eleven: Mount Sequoia, the very blades of grass in my yard, my little shingled house on Rush Drive. The things of place: bagworms on the bushes, back door that stuck, the casement window the maple loved to brush against.

Words themselves have to keep brushing against their objects, Wendell Berry says. Language becomes precise only in its constant testing against objects. And we can only know words as they relate to the whole "household" in which they occur. We must know where we are. Dante speaks in first person, Berry reminds us. Holding himself within those limits, he makes his created world credible. Milton, on the other hand, speaking omnisciently, "reduces omnipotence to a matter of chariots and weapons."

The movers carry our boxes into our new house. We are back in the Midwest. I lovingly unpack the dishes, unwrap my desk lamp, the carved wooden cat, as if I had struck gold. I would like to think I can be myself without accoutrements, but even the homeless push grocery carts full of their small tokens. I would like to think I'm myself without titles or recognitions, but even unvoiced, they speak. Certain of my neurons have collected the details and spoken to each other simultaneously so often that between their separate synapses, they've given birth to memory. Memory is made of synapses grown comfortable with each other.

All the people who retire to places they've loved—it isn't the past they find. But the past stirs inside the present there. It can be felt, the way one's parents and grandparents gradually rise in one's face, in one's body. To return to a place is to put oneself at the intersection of past and present, where the energy, for good or ill, is surging.

I am twelve. There is my father, muscles tensed and flexing, raging in the kitchen. "We'll starve this summer," he yells. "If we can't stop spending all my salary over the winter, we deserve to starve!" He insists on keeping an academic year pay schedule. There is my small mother, her delicate bones, huddled in a chair, sobbing. What has she done—bought some name brands instead of store brands? A new bedspread? Nothing much. She weakly defends herself. She can't counter the rage that rises from his depths. It feels barely controlled, murderous. I try to focus on her, to see what she looks like, what she says in her defense. She's wearing a pink sweat shirt with hearts on it. Her dark hair is long, like he likes it, her pony tail falling over one shoulder. I can see her but I can't hear her. They are in the same room, in the same life, somehow inextricably here, lost in their sorrow and their rage. She wants to be a child again, safe in her parents' house. She is a child. He is a wild animal, helplessly raging through the bars of his own cage. I hold them here. They don't see me holding them here. They don't see themselves, either.

The rage of my father's life rises as stubbornly in me as my memory of his box kites, the ones he made himself out of grocery bags and balsa sticks, that flew so high they were just specks with long, long tails. No one else could get a kite that high and that stable. It just sat up there like a pencil point, delicate and glorious, and I was holding the string that barely tethered earth to sky.

He would take me on his motor scooter out in the country to fly his model planes, the ones he designed and built himself. Not remote control, but controlled so well from aileron and wing position that they remarkably obeyed. He tinkered, adjusted. His focus is still brilliant. Watch him start a difficult motor. He puts his face down to it. He listens for its particular tics, he chokes it, feeds it gas as if it were an extension of his own body. No motor fails to run for him. If one fails, he remakes it, rewinds its copper coils. I am the one watching, invisible, awed. I learn all I can, to get smart enough so that he might turn my way.

I get smarter and smarter. I am a smart aleck. I think up ways to provoke him. I say I'm always going to spend lots of money and never save anything. I say all my friends have more clothes than I do (which is true). I say I don't care if I understand the math, I only want to get the right answer and get a good grade. We rage at each other. I will not be my mother, if I can help it. His rage is bigger than mine. He sets his jaw. "You must be a complete idiot," he says. I bury my face in a pillow and cry.

While I'm in my room with the door slammed, I'll have him head down to the basement to work on his boat. He's designed and built five sailboats. He's bent the wood for the hulls, soaked the boards in creosote himself to preserve them, cut and bent his own sail track slides, cut and sewed his own sails. You'd think he'd be pleased that he did this, proud of it. All he says is that he just wanted to sail, and he couldn't afford to do it any other way. He says he cared nothing about the process. There's this in him, a kind of cauterized part. He likes to look at the shape of the hull, though. He used to say he'd like to get on a sailboat and sail forever—alone, except he'd like a woman with him, for sex (He didn't say my mother, particularly). There I was, left behind.

Another detail: when I was seven or eight, he carved a huge propeller for the back of his bike. He hooked it up to an old Briggs and Stratton motor and, after a few tries at different torques for the blade, he had a machine that worked wonderfully and cheaply. He tried to license it as a motorbike, but was told it had to have a protective guard over the blade. That would have made the whole rig too heavy, so he pedaled it beyond the city limits and then started the motor out in the country. Sometimes he took me. We'd fly down the road in the morning mist, me, gloriously happy, on the seat behind. I was a part of this, at least. But we had to halt for every dog, for fear the propeller would lop off its head. Dirt and rocks nibbled at the blade. He gave it up.

I'm in love with my words, with what they can make. I get to spinning along; I'm spinning out of control, building my sentences, adoring every minute of it, and then he'll be out of the picture again. I suppose the truth always gets away like that, shifting from particle to wave. And the closer we look, the more it shifts. Even in poems—the only poems I've written that I'm really happy with are the ones that opened up gaps where the truth would be if you could find it. It's a mystery how that happens. I can't say what the truth is, but if I get the words right, will they start to form a shape that might be the shape of it?

Or are my memories mostly nostalgia? Nostalgia is memory's whore, dressing up as whatever excites the emotions. By the time their interludes are over, memory has slipped out the door, taking with it the real darkness, the parts one wants to avoid. Maybe I pile up objects as a relief, something to hold onto. I fill the rooms with them even as I carry them out. Each room is a safe house.

The house we've just moved into is 110 years old. It's in the historic part of Traverse City: big trees, old-fashioned streetlights, front porches. After thirty years on the East Coast, it feels like Mayberry here, people walking their dogs, riding their bikes. Our house's mute history can be traced in its cracks, its plastered-in holes where doors used to be. We have a "Michigan basement," a dungeon of a space with huge, wide walls, excavated and concreted in after the fact. An uneasy stalemate between concrete and Michigan sand.

In an old house, you're aware of being in the middle, maintaining with your own life the boundary between the present time and the past owners' memories. In another dimension, those people inhabit the rooms, wash the dishes, lug baskets of clothes down to the washer. You can feel them, just out of reach. You wonder about them.

My father finished the annual hundred-mile bike club ride when he was almost eighty, on his old bike with only three gears. All those years he rode with the town bike club, the other riders were proud of him and wanted to be his friend. He was their oldest member—the local newspaper featured him in a story. When he got too old to pedal his bike up steep hills, they pooled their money to buy him a motor for it, but he refused their offer. He just quit riding, and quit seeing any of them. If one of the club members came by the house, he said he thought it was "odd" that they would keep "coming after him." Now he goes home from the Senior Center, reads and pounds on his typewriter, makes his supper out of the cheapest ingredients he can find, and eats it alone, unless his lady friend Rebecca is allowed to come over. I'll get to her.

I think of him always getting away, on his bike, sailing, taking long hikes, or leaning down over a clock that wouldn't run, probing its tiny cogs, his tongue protruding slightly from the side of his mouth. Always a space around him. He used to take my sister and me on bike rides, and then we would get off and he would carry one of us on his shoulders as we hiked along a creek bank. We had a good time. He could tell us the names of flowers and trees, and we watched for fish.

Memory begins in the hippocampus, most likely, then is transferred to other parts of the brain that will keep it safer. Who can understand the hippocampus? It gathers the dark, unspoken impulses of the amygdala, the translations of the thalamus, the excitations of the hypothalamus, signals from all over, and makes them into what we call memory, a reconstruction of names, faces, stories. Reconstruction, with all its errors.

Was there an original? As I flew down the road holding onto my father's waist, propeller roaring behind us, microseconds slipped away as fast as they happened. What is my original face? Who was my mother? Who is my father? I think he doesn't know. Existing is too hard: you don't want to disturb the universe that much. When his famous father was honored posthumously at the University of Missouri, several of the economics faculty of the school where my father taught went to Columbia to the ceremony, but my father didn't go because he didn't think he would be allowed time off from his classes. He didn't ask. One time he was sent to a conference in another city. He almost wore out his shoes walking miles and miles to and from the hotel because he didn't dare ask for money from his department for cab fare. I'm sure he felt he didn't deserve cab fare. He likes to say he doesn't deserve things. He says it if you offer him a piece of pie. "Oh, I don't know. I don't deserve it." He's both serious and ironic. But the truth is, he can't make decisions. And it is in choosing that we construct ourselves.

My sister and I used to sit on our twin beds, endlessly trying to unravel the strangenesses in our household. We were junior psychologists. Writing's done the same for me, of course. D. H. Lawrence said, "We shed our sicknesses in books." What am I doing this time, as I finger each of the details again? Trying to locate myself, to map the land I live on. Trying to more clearly see this man whose life is nearly over, who ought not to leave this world simplified by nostalgia or decorated by my own pleasurable experimentations with language. Who deserves to be seen the way God and Picasso would see him: from all angles, simultaneously, tenderly.

Another angle: my father looks and smells like a street person. He brushes his teeth with plain water. He showers using as little soap as possible. He uses bar soap on his hair. He doesn't use deodorant. His electric razor died, so he shaves with my mother's old one, which leaves patches of stubble all over his face. He washes his clothes once a week or so, the same clothes over and over. He wears a brown jacket he got at Goodwill that at one time was part of a UPS uniform. His grease-stained khaki pants have huge patches he's ironed and sewn onto the knees. Last summer when he was getting ready to be taken to the doctor, his rotten pants split all the way down the hips, and my sister had to scrounge up something of her husband's for him to wear. He had no other suitable pants. He won't let us buy him any. He says he wants to wear out what he has before he dies.

Another angle: his manners. He grew up in a highly civilized, intellectual family. There were dinner parties. He apparently loved and admired his parents, so his lack of manners doesn't seem to be rebellion. No, it's not lack of manners: it's a kind of outright defiance. If you sit across the table from him you can hardly eat, it's so sickening. He stuffs the food in. He talks with his mouth wide open, half-chewed food barely remaining inside, sometimes spilling out the sides. He makes noises as he chews. He acts like a three-year-old. If you tell him to close his mouth, he flies into a rage about the insanity of manners, the prissy delicacy of your stomach. He reminds you that he's not telling YOU how to eat. It's not worth it. Best shut your eyes.

Now I'm tipping over again, losing boundaries, getting lost in the weirdness of my father. Am I using his peculiarities, his ingenuity, to my writerly advantage, to enhance myself in the process? How do these inevitable filters affect what I try to see of him, just him? How much exactitude can a loving portrait contain, can love contain? And what's the right distance? I adjust the microscope. He took us swimming. He made us kites. He played with us, really played, with great joy. He was amazingly funny. He made up great and ghastly bedtime stories. He's always been a child.

It is a terror and a wild joy to be raised by a child. The world is always out of kilter, sliding out of control, but the sky sings with adventure and the depths are teeming with stories. The child of a child learns to tightrope-walk, fashion her own balance pole, make her own solid earth.

Suppose this essay were about, say, Brueghel. It would still be shaped by me, with my proclivities. What should I include, what leave out? I remember W. D. Snodgrass's term, *tact*, a restraint that keeps out of a poem the language that tells us how we should feel. He says Randall Jarrell "shows us what's required—a complete removal from any ulterior motive, an absolute dedication to the object and experience."

What's my motive? I would like not to have one. Like Brueghel, I would like to fill the canvas with dancers, color, darkness, and details. In William Gaddis's *The Recognitions*, one of the main characters has been obsessed with trying to understand how the Flemish painters were so open to vitality in all of its minute detail, leaving no space on the canvas free of the celebration of all of life. Toward the end of the novel, he "realizes" that his assumptions are all wrong: the Flemish painters were in fact afraid of emptiness, terrified that if they left even the smallest space vacant, everything would collapse in a void.

But there's another kind of space, I think, the kind that can open up *because of* the concentration of the work.

On the day my mother was buried, after we had all come home from the cemetery, my father took my son Scott and his cousin David into the bedroom to show them the device he uses to maintain an erection (Viagra doesn't work for him, he told me later). "I'll probably never get to use it again," he said to them, tearfully. This was his concern on the day of his wife's funeral. These were his grandchildren. Did he love my mother? Yes. He needed her. He needed someone to keep him company and someone to have sex with. He said as much, not quite in those words. I think she felt that, often. He declares that this is pretty much what human relationship is. My father never visits my mother's grave. It makes no logical sense to visit a grave, he says. But, yes, he loved her, even if his demonstrations of it seemed

as though he were an actor, saying his lines, reluctantly be-
having in a way others would perceive as "normal." I heard
him say once that "Rebecca couldn't hold a candle to your
mother." Or something like that.

After my mother died, as soon as the air cleared, my father
was down at the Senior Center scouting out a new woman.
Within a few months, he'd narrowed the possibilities to two.
He picked Rebecca, the one who was sure to give him the
least trouble. Not an attractive or strong woman, she was
madly in love with him in a short time. Did he love her? Does
he love her now as she slides off into her final dementia?
They've had ten years of good companionship. He's picked
her up almost every evening and brought her to his house,
where they've eaten dinner together. Her daughter Marie
tried to understand her mother's new life, but my father's
social awkwardness and horrific personal habits no doubt
set her against him pretty quickly.

He has always been good to Rebecca. He's been kind and
patient. He's paid for the food for their dinners. On Sundays
he's taken her to a (cheap) restaurant. Yet he often speaks
as if she were an object. One of the first things he said about
her to me is that Rebecca is "not smart, for sure." Also, Rebecca has always had colitis, and he describes in detail her
loss of control. He would describe their sex life in detail if
I'd let him. Years ago, I blew up at him and forbade him to
discuss sex with me. To him, it's just another fact.

Essays with breaks in them, sentences with no verbs, mirror-
ing the brain's image-shifts, the nonsequiturs of the memory world we all inhabit beneath and around the one we try
to keep stable enough to live in. Television shows, movie
trailers, and commercials flit and flash from image to image, leaving impressions, as if, well, the world is inexplicable, and the best we can do is, like, like, you know, like this,
trust the gaps, as in poems, to admit a truth unavailable
any other way. Or, there is no truth, only these atoms of experience. I wonder, though, if it's not an evasion, also, a re-
fusal to concentrate like Flemish painters, to consciously
work toward connection, to find the conjunctions, the tran-
sitions, that commit to a point of view, and, once committed, accept the consequences of that choice.

Rebecca's daughter Marie and her husband used to invite
my father to their family gatherings. Now Rebecca is worse
and has to live with them, and they don't want him around.
They don't drive him away, but they're rude and dismissive.
I can't get an accurate picture of things, because I hear it all
from him. I'm sure they never wanted him there, and now
they have more control. Here's a man who, although he may
be more educated, is dirty, cheap, and doesn't conform to
any social expectations. He doesn't send Rebecca flowers,
he doesn't buy her scarves or bracelets. My Nana, mother's

mother, used to say "They broke the mold when they made you, Phillips." That was the Christian in her, trying not to hate him for that something, that empty spot at the core that made him seem at times other than human.

Rebecca got sick and Marie wouldn't let him near her or even tell him how she was doing. He panicked. He wrote Marie a letter hoping to find out something, hoping to gain admittance again. He read it to me on the phone. It compared his position with Rebecca's family to the relationship of the West to Kim Il Jong, the totalitarian leader of North Korea, and expressed his doubt that Rebecca's doctor was right in assuming she had a virus and not giving her an antibiotic (Marie's husband is a nurse). Thank God I stopped him from sending it.

Speaking of God, my father does so with great regularity. He is in love with disproving the existence of God. My childhood was more saturated with God-talk than most preachers' kids'. He knew the arguments: his father had made him read Herbert Spencer, Darwin, Huxley, and all the scientific materialists as a boy. As I got older, I began to see that his arguments repeated themselves with no development. He describes the fundamentalist position and demolishes it, over and over. He seems unable to understand metaphor at all. I gave him Joseph Campbell. He was baffled. He's confounded (and thus a little angered) by words like "spirit," "ecstasy," or "transcendence." For all his wide reading, he never reads fiction.

I used to think his family had stunted and repressed his emotional side, but they were from all appearances loving. His parents spent probably a fortune to send his sailboat to him by train while he was at Harvard, so he could sail it there. He wrote funny and loving letters home. He wrote quite charming romantic poems as a young man. Although he's an economist and sees the world through rigorously theoretical lenses, he cries at the suffering of the poor he sees on television. He even cries at soap operas, or used to before he gave them up as a waste of time. Yet this is what he has said about my sisters and me: "I suppose it's natural to care more about your children, since they carry your genes. I can't see any other reason." He can remember the names of post office clerks from forty years ago, but he can't recall incidents from my childhood that are specifically about me. He's always glad to hear from me, but I have to call him. He won't spend the money. He sends long, single-spaced typed letters—sometimes six or eight pages or more. "Dear_____," he often writes, filling in each daughter's name on the line after he's made copies. They're really letters to a deaf universe, about politics, religion, the furnace motor, and his allergies.

Ah, but there's an astounding disconnect in him. He is so glad to see us that he almost cries. And I am convinced he deeply misses my mother. It is as if mind and body are

utterly, irrevocably separated, east and west, each yearning for the other, unable to reach across.

Concentration can lead down into one's fears. It was a fear-
ful house I grew up in. My father was, and is, almost constantly afraid. Panic is closer to the right word. You can still
hear it in his voice most of the time. When we were young,
he was afraid of (1) running out of money; (2) the car breaking down: (3) bosses, policemen; (4) not getting enough
sex; (5) not finishing his dissertation and losing his job; (6)
not getting his boat finished because of lack of time and
money; (7) losing things; (8) anything, you name it, in the
house breaking down. His ear was constantly tuned toward
glitches in the smooth running of machinery. It was always
only a matter of time, for him.

When we lose something, who knows how much of our grief
is panic? What now? I write this in an unfamiliar town. My
old life is dead. None of my reflexes apply. I admit, I'm a
little afraid. Not to mention that I've come one step closer
to dying.

Our friends on the East Coast imagine us living out here in a
vast Siberian wasteland. How can you live without the Met,
the Philadelphia Orchestra, the Smithsonian, large research
universities at your fingertips? What will you do? They don't
say this. My guess is, they think we're burying ourselves

before we die, that we've chosen to sit on the porch and knit. Not so bad, they say, but it's not where Life is.

Where does one go to find life? There is only the vertical, only the awareness of each moment, even as it gathers its own version of past and future to itself.

The moment always contains a longing, a Something missing. You can't help but return, go over and over things, to figure out what it is. It's not reasons we're looking for. It's my belief that we could get to the bottom of it, we could find a reason for everything that happens, if we knew enough. If we had enough of the facts. If we could add up enough details, even Jesus raising Lazarus from the dead could be rationally explained. But an explanation of how things happen isn't the same as what I guess I'll call mystery. Mystery stands outside of knowledge. It's not a gap in perception or an error. I am a mystery to myself. Those I love are a mystery to me. No matter how deeply I know them, the sum of who they are is greater. The spark of connection between the identifiable, explicable elements ignites the conflagration we've named the soul.

It was my son Scott who first said, "I think Granddaddy's a little autistic." After all these years, a word. Asperger's Syndrome, most likely. Here are some of the characteristics of Asperger's I can easily match to my father:

- Inability to pick up on social cues, lacking inborn social skills, such as being able to read others' body language, start or maintain a conversation, and take turns talking.

- May appear to lack empathy.

- A preoccupation with one or only few interests, which he or she may be very knowledgeable about. May be overly interested in parts of a whole or in unusual activities, such as doing intricate jigsaw puzzles, designing houses, drawing highly detailed scenes, or astronomy.

- Has a preference for sameness, routine.

- Talks a lot, usually about a favorite subject. One-sided conversations are common. Thoughts are often verbalized with no filter.

- Overreacts to things that other people would not react to at all.

- Sometimes has an awkward walk.

- Often has advanced rote memorization and math skills. Is able to memorize dates, formulas, and phone numbers in unusually accurate detail.

Would it have made a difference if I'd known this earlier? No one had named this gathering of traits until the year I was born (1944), when a Viennese physician, Hans Asperger, published a paper that described a pattern of behaviors in several young boys who had normal (often high) intelligence and language development, but who also exhibited autistic-like behaviors and marked deficiencies in social and communication skills. His paper was published in the 1940s, but it wasn't until 1994 that Asperger's Syndrome was added to the DSM IV, and only in the past few years has it been generally recognized by professionals and the public.

"Oh, it's Daddy's Asperger's." I guess that would have helped. A little autistic. He's probably a little autistic. Probably, but who knows for sure? There's relief, a sense of arrival, when you find a word that feels like the right one. But words are like image flashes on a screen—they give a facile sense of seeing. They convince you that you "know" something. Eventually scientists will identify the exact glitch in the brain that's responsible, and possibly find a way to fix it. Maybe they'll find the location of empathy and enhance it. I recognize my father in me, though, when I turn my thoughts in this direction. I make the issue about naming and fixing. The intangible human being gets absorbed into language, gets lost.

When my sister Melinda was in a coma after her brain tumor was removed, he said if he could die now and that would guarantee that she would live, he'd do it.

Has he been happy? He's utterly unconcerned with the word, but if pressed, he'll say he has been, and is. Though I see, in spite of his laughter, his wonderful whistling, his long sails in a good wind, so much loss, so much loneliness, so much panic, fear, and frustration. I'll grant him his view, but my evidence points to a different conclusion. My conclusion is mine, of course, encompassing much more than the individual mind of my father. Who knows what channels may lie in his mind that lead away from the pain and toward the joy? He's smart enough to have figured how to carve them.

One side of my father's basement is now clean. There's still the freezer with decades-old frozen food in it. He says he'll clean that out, but he won't. There's the rest of the house, but little by little we'll get to it. Stuff will be gone. He will be gone. I will be gone. Memory will disappear.

Coda: She looks at a photo of her father, gorgeously nineteen or twenty, headed down a wooded path, legs of his overalls flapping, shit-grin, shirtsleeves rolled like a workman's, pen in pocket. Has he been lonely since? Is he satisfied? The daisies along the path, the slight blur of trees overhead, make her ache: that moment, charged with before and after, the father who is not yet a father (assuming there's a stable self, assuming that everything starts someplace: say, the word *Father*). She wants to pin down a beginning, a trajectory, a "once" that gives birth to an end. No matter if it comes down to *Father forgive them*. And

there's her father, his bent old body, pinioned by itself, con-
stipated, heart aided by stent. The path, if there was a path,
got made by the making. What was cleared, or cleared away?
Is he stepping through? Who can she turn to, who could be
the everything and nothing that made her? That moment
of pure delight?

Soft Conversations

I partly blame my excruciating earaches. They would punch inward toward the brain and pound like a frantic drummer against the tender roots of my senses. In the fifties, when I was in grade school, there were no antihistamines yet. My sinuses would fill and get infected; my ears would be next. I would lie in bed with a heating pad turned up so high my ear would turn fiery red. I would wrench myself into a ball and sob with pain. As with childbirth, I've forgotten exactly how it felt, only the tone, the wild isolation of it, the sweet smell of the heating pad, of hot flesh, of sweat. I would be taken to the doctor, who would lance my eardrum to let the pressure out. Scar tissue, over and over, that toughened the eardrum, leaving it less resilient.

Then there was the BB gun I shot with the man who became my first husband, knocking beer cans off rocks. Bam, bam, no ear protection. Then years later, with an ex-Vietnam sniper, the .44, a fierce gun, fiercely loud. With only cotton in my ears, I shot at water-filled plastic jugs. Even then I could imagine the cilia in my middle ear breaking off like mown wheat.

Maybe none of the above influenced the inevitable. Grandfather Brown always said, "Come around to my good side," his left ear virtually deaf for years. My uncle Bob wears hearing aids in both ears. His sister my mother wore hearing aids in both ears—obvious, awkward things that indiscriminately amplified all sounds and left her at the mercy of my loud father and a room reverberating with children and grandchildren. All she could do was turn them off and tune out, which she frequently did.

Soft conversation as if from another room. The cadence of frustration, of anger, shed of specifics. The rhythm of a line, playing off a nice, entirely safe, entirely unreachable iambic base. More like a poem to her: the tone of it, the impact below meaning, blow of meaning in the stomach.

Needless to say, my hearing is not good. My left ear's the main culprit; at every pitch, the dots on the hearing test graph describe a deep droop below the normal line. (My right ear's dots, for now, rest right on the line.) There is nothing to be done for the left one except amplify with a hearing aid. A tiny, expensive digital hearing aid works well for me, for now. When I say it works well, I don't mean really well. You can only amplify vibrations the ear is still able to register. Some crucial pitches are lost forever, usually the high ones first, the tiny fillips that distinguish between one word and another. It's the same as if the tops of some letters have been sliced off. Your chances of guessing right are good, but not perfect. I've changed over to my right ear for phone conversations, because even with the hearing aid, the left ear has to work too hard. But I think of D. H. Lawrence's description of Dorothy Brett with her huge horn held to the ear, straining to hear anything. I think of my husband's story of his uncle Evans, battery pack almost as large as a Gideon bible in his shirt pocket, cord snaking up to one ear, Jerry riding along with him in his little Crosley, his uncle's shouting drowning out even the noisy engine. And my mother, with her two hearing aids, wincing in loud rooms, wincing at the feedback when we leaned in to kiss her hello. I'm grateful for the Tom Thumb–sized digital hearing aid that can be programmed to amplify selectively for one's weaknesses.

God, I should be grateful to be alive. People are being bombed to death in trains in Spain, crushed by earthquakes in Italy, riddled with bullets in Iraq, starving all over, being beaten to death all over. Each small loss, each seeping away of powers, however gentle, to the body, to the spirit, is like the Victorian's skull on the bedside table, a reminder. No one is exempt.

Hearing, when it goes, usually seeps away slowly; the mind adjusts, increment by increment. People start refusing to be clear. You hear a low male voice and think you're fine. Then a soft, wispy voice, and you don't know why she can't speak up. Or maybe you lost concentration for a moment. You feel irked at yourself, too. If I had to choose, I guess I'd prefer to lose hearing instead of sight. But that's probably because sight is so obvious, its loss so easy to feel. I close my eyes and the world disappears. But then I block my ears. What cottony land is this, without birdcalls, music, my children's jokes, my husband's mellow everyday talk? Sound is what we swim in.

Actually, it swims in us. I picture it knocking against the eardrum, the knocking's contraction and expansion swinging into motion the tiny bones of the hammer, anvil, and stirrup on the other side. The stirrup starts the fluid in the middle ear vibrating. The farther in, the more swimming, deep into the cochlea, filled with fluid, its inner surface touchy with over 20,000 hairy nerve cells. As a wave moves through them, they begin to rock, each one with its own natural sensitivity to a particular vibration. When the wave matches the natural frequency of the nerve cell, dancer and dance become indistinguishable. The whole resonates with a larger vibration, triggering the cell to release an electrical impulse. I can see tadpoles of electricity swimming along the auditory nerve toward the brain, but after that, the brain takes them in, closes the door against me, and dances its mysterious dance into consciousness.

Yesterday evening there was a loon in the middle of the lake. I paddled my little kayak to within twenty feet of it and sat waiting for its ancient call. Long silence, then it lifted its black beak and gave out from the depths, *ooo-wah-hoo*: quavering, powerful, once, then again silence, floating. The loon and my ear did their dance together, then let go.

Vibration—the rhythm of energy—is what carries us, what is us. If we could pay attention enough, we'd see we're nothing but vibration, even to ourselves. There's no letting go, really, after the loon cry, only a shift in pitch, in tone, in the soup of sounds. It's the breaks in attention that make us— and the world—appear to be solid, appear to have a beginning and an end. All classic science depends upon breaks in attention. Geometry, line, sequence, and identity are carved out of what would be a continuum, if we could look steadily enough. Words, too, each one fighting for its territory, yearning for what it tries to stand for. I'm not sorry to have the appearance of solidity, the bird song, the code, break, break, the hey-hey of the words.

Last night there was a bird—not a loon—I kept hearing over and over: sharp, resolved, long interval between, unlike anything—a singularity, as if all bird sounds were compressed into one. It seemed like the night itself. Now it's dawn and here they all go, the wrens' *tea-kettle, tea-kettle,* tea-kettle, the cardinals' *cheer-cheer-cheer, what-what-what-what*, the chickadees' *fee-bee-ee*, the nuthatches' nasal *ah-ah, ah-ah*, galaxies of sound shrinking and expanding in the trees, certain males out to prove after a night's hunting that they still have energy for love. What they have to say otherwise is beyond me. Their voices radiate outward, sharp as little jewels. I watch their hollow bones lift them closer to heaven than I am. Closer, because they take themselves for what they are, without cunning, not a trope among them. Yet in ten minutes, a male can counterfeit the dialect of a territory and make himself available to its females. Even this deception seems direct, honestly purposeful.

Bird sound comes from the syrinx, a membrane lower in the throat than our vocal cords, at the junction of two air tubes leading to the lungs. So there are two sound sources, one in each bronchus, two separate sounds that mix and feed into the higher vocal tract. For this reason, birds can make many more sounds than I can. They seem never to breathe, but actually they take shallow minibreaths, synchronized with the rich syllables of song.

We call them rich if sound waves have a whole-number mathematical relationship between them. The more frequencies, the more complex the waves. If there's no simple mathematical relationship between the frequencies, we call it noise. The clatter, for example, of a pencil striking the floor. Or tanks coming into Tikrit, their guns going pop, pop, pop, pop. No relationship of frequencies, no relation to relationship.

Gyuto Monks are able to make two or three chords simultaneously when they're in samadhi, a trancelike state of pure consciousness. During the Mahakala Offering ritual, there's a moment in the chant when the monks visualize millions of "music deities" streaming forth from the mandala, blessing the world's people and pleasing the world's deities by performing every conceivable type of music known to men and gods. *Om mani padmi hum. Om* centers the mind and body, calls them home; *mani padmi*, translated as the jewel in the heart of the lotus, is the eardrum of the universe, the place where all flowering begins, and is gathered; *hum* calls the mind to attention. One snaps that last syllable. One is there, aware of being there.

There I am, at a party, at attention among the buzz of voices. The shapes of words become crucial, the context, the lip and body movements. I lean in, greedy for clues. Flit? Fidget? Licorice? What were we talking about that one of these words would fit? And there I am in bed with my husband. I turn on one side, his voice softens to a muddy lull from a far distance. This is a little scary, losing touch. I turn over, and there he is again. I am home.

The tones we call pure are the ones that vibrate at a single frequency. A flute is an example. If I had a pure, essential sound that is me, I wonder what it would be. Sound isn't personal, really, only air blowing against something, except that pitch is regulated by the shape that directs the air. The sound itself is code, a *dot-dot-dash* in the airflow, a stop and start, a particular pattern. Nothing is personal at the core. It's when we combine elements that we begin to infuse them with emotion, with personality. I have some of my mother's intonations. I can hear her calling me. "Flee-duh. FLEE-duh!" She's been dead seven years, yet the sound of her voice is reproduced in my head exactly as if I were six years old and it's time for dinner. I long to stay outside, yet I'm relieved to be called in, glad for the precious few limits that she sets on my freedom. Her voice sounds as if she's worked to get it out, as if she isn't sure she has the right to demand anything. The inner sounds stay and stay as my hearing wanes. They attach themselves to my emotions, and memory translates them into a different text, maybe into particles instead of waves, like the *x*'s and *o*'s of a computer program.

I admit I don't listen well. My father's ranting, arguing, lecturing most of his waking hours, swallowed all the space around him. And if your parents fight a lot, you learn how to shut your ears. I can make a sound disappear. Years ago, I began to have tinnitus, at first a mild ringing in the ears, then loud, persistent, announcing increasing nerve damage. Gradually I turned the ringing into background. I have cicadas inside my head. Not cicadas, exactly: too deep for identification, too steady for messages. But not wallpaper. A small anguish, or a big one heard at a far distance, one I can't fix, so I try to ignore it.

Unfortunately, though, sounds I want to hear also disappear. For a poet, I'm a poor listener to poems. When I read them, I hear them well in my head, but when they're spoken I have to concentrate harder than most just to hang on. The habit of my ears is to turn away. The habit of my mind and my ears is to turn away, to drift. The drifting, however pleasant, is as dangerous as drifting in a boat. For a little while, it's fun. But then it gets dangerous. You can hit something. You can get lost. You can die never having lived your real, singular life.

The singular voice that belongs to me exists only when it gets drawn into the galaxy-shaped whorl of someone's ear and spins down to the eardrum. I'm a combination of pitches, a center around which a definition of self gathers—the same gesture the whole universe makes, things thrown out by the big bang, or drawn inward by the Great Attractor at unimaginable speed. Curving, at any rate, moving through a curved universe.

Waves or particles, depending. Sound, for instance, is made up of both the rocking ocean of itself and also of tiny iambics, trochaics, wavelets on its surface—pinpricks in the atmosphere, or in the consciousness. Years ago, my husband's therapist, trying to help him get past his anger at his father, told him to listen with his left ear, to hear emotions, to hear his own father's loss and sadness. Interestingly, it seems to work, at least for those of us who are right-handed. The left side is the quiet side, the one less interested in butting in, or shaping the conversation, the one that hears cadence, stress, the ocean of the feelings. My right ear hears my mother's voice in pinpricks of actual words; my left ear hears her sorrow, regret, longing, even her joy. Once my daughter said to me, "You have no idea how powerful anything you say is, to my ear." The damage my words do, the good they do, I can only guess.

For sheer, brute power, we usually speak louder, more slowly. When we want communal power, the tendency is to compress, to intensify, to ritualize into chant, poetry, song. When we're sad, song drives worries out through the vocal cords, the body translating instead of allowing the brain to keep circling like an old donkey around a post. When we're happy—I know no sound as compelling as whistling. My father was glorious at it, before he had a bridge that changed the dynamics of his mouth. He would fool around in the garden, tying up tomatoes, whistling snatches of Beethoven,

of Dvořák. I would feel, for those moments, a mighty release, an ease. I was flying like a bird. There was nothing
but that moment, and I was glad to be alive in it. Whistling
doesn't register long-range happiness or sadness. It regis-
ters our presence in this blessed life.

Then about the time you think you have yourself located
in this life, separated out, you begin to take on the family
infirmities that insist on including you as part of a whole.
I look at my face in the mirror, more and more my mother's. I buy my hearing aid. I hate it that I can't escape, but I
hear my mother calling me in to dinner, and again, I'm relieved, in a bittersweet way, that there are limits to everything, that I am attached to the earth, that I will die. It is, after all, our inexorable mortality that brings us together. In
the summers, my daughter, my sisters, and I do water ballet together, at our age. It's even sillier than that: one night
every summer, we attach tiny headlights on stretch bands
on our heads. We call ourselves the Headlight Sisterhood,
and we swim at night, nude, under the stars, singing songs
with the word light in them, "This little light of mine," and
so on. It is exactly our separate sorrows, each one a small,
flashing signal of mortality, that creates a sisterhood, that
gives us our singing.

Over our heads, around us, trillions of radio waves, if we
could count them, are bouncing off satellites by the minute.

The air is thick with them. The air is thick with what we can't hear unless we have the right receiver. How glib it would be to make a moral out of that. The world is a complicated and noisy party, and we are all straining to hear what we can. We miss a lot. Sometimes we deliberately arrange for a little deafness. There's sound all the time, everywhere, and we have to artificially clump it up to make it work for us. We leave rests, caesuras, to make music and poetry possible. It's the hush between words that gives them their integrity.

And still, even after the hush, they're never quite what we'd hoped—the quavers and sliding quivers struggling to relate to each other, leaving an aching loss when they can't quite. The word Buddhists use for this, the ancient Pali word, is *dukkha*, often translated as suffering, but it means something deeper, a basic unsatisfactoriness that runs though our lives. Things are never quite perfect. "But . . . ," we start to say, rushing to balance the scales, to say what's good about it, dooming ourselves to addition and subtraction. Meanwhile, the trillion radio waves, the trillion, trillion stars wink in and out of our consciousness, seen and unseen, dark and light, depending utterly upon each other, neither plus nor minus.

Books by Fleda Brown

Poetry

Reunion (University of Wisconsin Press, 2007)

Breathing In, Breathing Out (Anhinga Press, 2002)

The Women Who Loved Elvis All Their Lives (Carnegie Mellon University Press, 2004)

The Devil's Child* (Carnegie Mellon University Press, 1999)

The Earliest House* (Kutztown University, 1994)

The Eleusinian Mysteries MS* (The Moment Press, 1992)

Do Not Peel the Birches* (Purdue University Press, 1993)

Fishing with Blood* (Purdue University Press, 1988)

Edited Volumes

Coeditor, with Billie Travalini, On the Mason-Dixon Line: An Anthology of Contemporary Delaware Writers (University of Delaware Press, 2007)

Coeditor, with Dennis Jackson, Critical Essays on D. H. Lawrence* (G. K. Hall, 1988)

---

*as Fleda Brown Jackson

In the American Lives series

Fault Line
by Laurie Alberts

Pieces from Life's Crazy Quilt
by Marvin V. Arnett

Songs from the Black Chair
A Memoir of Mental Illness
by Charles Barber

Driving with Dvořák
Essays on Memory and Identity
by Fleda Brown

Searching for Tamsen Donner
by Gabrielle Burton

American Lives
A Reader
edited by Alicia Christensen
introduced by Tobias Wolff

Out of Joint
A Private & Public Story of
Arthritis
by Mary Felstiner

Falling Room
by Eli Hastings

Opa Nobody
by Sonya Huber

Hannah and the Mountain
Notes toward a Wilderness
Fatherhood
by Jonathan Johnson

Local Wonders
Seasons in the Bohemian Alps
by Ted Kooser

Bigger than Life
A Murder, a Memoir
by Dinah Lenney

What Becomes You
by Aaron Raz Link and Hilda Raz

Turning Bones
by Lee Martin

In Rooms of Memory
Essays
by Hilary Masters

Between Panic and Desire
by Dinty W. Moore

Thoughts from a Queen-Sized Bed
by Mimi Schwartz

The Fortune Teller's Kiss
by Brenda Serotte

Gang of One
Memoirs of a Red Guard
by Fan Shen

Just Breathe Normally
by Peggy Shumaker

Scraping By in the Big Eighties
by Natalia Rachel Singer

In the Shadow of Memory
by Floyd Skloot

Secret Frequencies
A New York Education
by John Skoyles

Phantom Limb
by Janet Sternburg

Yellowstone Autumn
A Season of Discovery in a Won-
drous Land
by W. D. Wetherell

To order or obtain more information on these or other University of Nebraska Press titles, visit www.nebraskapress.unl.edu.